IQ AND PSYCHOMETRIC TESTS

CENTREX
DEVELOPING POLICING EXCELLENCE

IQ AND PSYCHOMETRIC TESTS

ASSESS YOUR PERSONALITY, APTITUDE AND INTELLIGENCE

Philip Carter

KOGAN
PAGE

London and Sterling, VA

Whilst the author has made every effort to ensure that the content of this book is accurate, please note that occasional errors can occur in books of this kind. If you suspect that an error has been made in any of the tests included in this book, please inform the publishers at the address printed below so that it can be corrected at the next reprint.

First published in Great Britain and the United States in 2004

120 Pentonville Road
London N1 9JN
United Kingdom
www.kogan-page.co.uk

22883 Quicksilver Drive
Sterling VA 20166–2012
USA

British Library Cataloguing in Publication Data

A CIP record for this book is available from the British Library.

ISBN 0 7494 4118 6

Typeset by Saxon Graphics Ltd, Derby
Printed and bound in Great Britain by Clays Ltd, St Ives plc

Contents

Introduction

The aim of this book is first and foremost to entertain, but at the same time stretch and exercise your mind, and to help you identify your own particular strengths and weaknesses, by means of a wide variety and scope of tests and exercises.

As defined by the British Psychological Society, a psychometric test is *an instrument designed to produce a quantitative assessment of some psychological attribute or attributes*. Such tests are basically tools for measuring the mind and are frequently used by employers as part of their selection process, to assist them in providing an accurate assessment of whether an individual is able to do the required job and whether the person's character is suited to the work. A meaning of the word 'metric' is measure, and 'psycho' means mind.

The two main types of psychometric tests used are aptitude tests and personality questionnaires. Aptitude tests, which include ability and intelligence tests, are designed to assess a person's abilities in a specific or general area, while personality questionnaires help to build up a profile of an individual's characteristics and personality.

In contrast to specific proficiencies or aptitudes, intelligence tests (IQ tests) are a standardized examination devised to measure human intelligence as distinct from attainments. Such a test consists of a series of questions, exercises and/or tasks which have been set to many thousands of examinees, and an average IQ of 100, known as the norm, has been worked out.

On the other hand a personality test is, by definition, designed to assess personality characteristics and/or forecast interpersonal difficulties. In addition, some of these tests try to measure problem-solving ability and determine whether you have the potential to supervise others.

To enable you to identify your strengths and weaknesses, the tests in this book have been divided into chapters, each of which is designed to give an objective assessment of abilities in a number of different disciplines, for example in verbal under-standing, numeracy, logical reasoning, technical aptitude and lateral thinking. Chapter 8 consists of two complete IQ tests which bring together all the different disciplines tested in the previous seven chapters.

There are also separate chapters devoted to creativity, memory tests and tests of personality.

It is now recognized that there are many different types of intelligence and that a high IQ, although desirable, is not the only key to success. Other characteristics such as outstanding artistic, creative or practical prowess, especially if combined with personal characteristics such as ambition, good temperament and compassion, could result in an outstanding level of success despite a low measured IQ. It is because of this that in recent years CQ (Creative Quotient) and EQ (Emotional Quotient), for example, have come to be regarded as equally important as, or even more important than, IQ measurement.

It must also be pointed out that having a high IQ does not mean that one has a good memory. A good memory is yet another type of intelligence, and could result in high academic success despite a low measured IQ. Someone with a rare combi-nation of a high IQ, good memory, self-discipline and dedi-cation is likely to become a very high flyer indeed.

Verbal intelligence tests

Test 1: Synonym test

A synonym is a word that has the same meaning as, or a very similar meaning to, another word. Examples of synonyms are: calm and placid, error and mistake, select and choose. This test is a series of 20 questions designed to test your knowledge of language and your ability to identify quickly words that have the same or very similar meanings.

You have 30 minutes to complete the 20 questions. You should work as quickly as possible as some questions will take more time to solve than others.

Questions 1 to 5

In the following five questions select the word in brackets that means the same or has the closest meaning to the word in capitals.

1. BRUSQUE (crude, curt, unkind, elastic, wieldy)

2. DISTIL (reduce, liquefy, soften, purify, rarefy)

3. SINGULAR (remarkable, free, routine, natural, upright)

4.   FASTIDIOUS (chic, loyal, protective, choosy, viable)

5.   WAX (souse, fade, shrink, strengthen, dilate)

Questions 6 to 10

In the following five questions, from the six words given identify the two words that you believe to be closest in meaning.

6.   flawless, ulterior, unwelcome, secret, overt, literate

7.   circle, row, pedal, track, flaw, line

8.   relative, common, exoteric, indolent, careless, apposite

9.   ascribe, profess, aspire, judge, hanker, daze

10. vote, composite, blend, proposition, element, total

Questions 11 to 20

The following are a miscellaneous selection of question types where, in each case, you have to identify two words with similar meanings. Read the instructions to each question carefully.

11. Complete the two words, one in each circle and both reading clockwise, which are similar in meaning. You have to find the starting point and provide the missing letters.

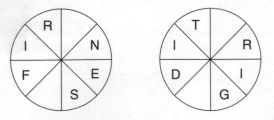

12. Complete the two words, one in each circle and both reading clockwise, which are similar in meaning. You have to find the starting point and provide the missing letters.

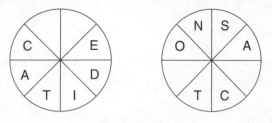

13. Complete the two words, one in each circle, one reading clockwise and the other anti-clockwise, that are similar in meaning. You have to find the starting point and provide the missing letters, and work out which word is clockwise and which is anti-clockwise.

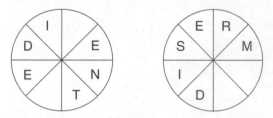

14. Which two words below are most similar to the phrase 'get the wrong idea'?

misconceive, miscalculate, misconstrue, misinform, misapply, misconduct

15. Which two words below are most similar to the phrase 'put in a good word for'?

conciliate, recommend, pacify, advise, endorse, enliven

16. Which two words below are most similar to the phrase 'down-to-earth'?

    subservient, dismayed, practical, earthward, explicit, realistic

17. ROPE OF CREW is an anagram of which two words (5, 5 letters) that are similar in meaning?

18. VINCIBLE OIL is an anagram of which two words (4, 7 letters) that are similar in meaning?

19. Each square contains the letters of a nine-letter word. Find the two words, one in each square, that are similar in meaning:

N	M	O		
U	E	G		
O	O	L	L	O
		Y	U	O
		Q	S	I

20. The circles contain the letters of two eight-letter words which can be found reading clockwise. Find the two words, which are similar in meaning. Each word starts in a different circle, and all letters appear in the correct order and are used once only.

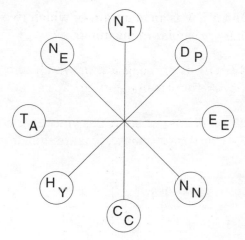

Answers to Test 1

1. curt
2. purify
3. remarkable
4. choosy
5. dilate
6. ulterior, secret
7. row, line
8. relative, apposite
9. aspire, hanker
10. composite, blend
11. firmness, rigidity
12. accredit, sanction
13. sediment, residuum
14. misconceive, misconstrue
15. recommend, endorse
16. practical, realistic
17. power, force
18. bill, invoice
19. monologue, soliloquy
20. tendency, penchant

Assessment

Each correct answer scores one point.

8–10   Average
11–13   Good
14–16   Very good
17–20   Exceptional

Test 2: Antonym test

An antonym is a word with the opposite meaning to another of the same language. Examples of antonyms are big and small, careless and heedful, happy and sad. This test is a series of 20 questions designed to test your knowledge of language and your ability to identify quickly words that have opposite meanings.

You have 40 minutes to complete the 20 questions. You should work as quickly as possible as some questions will take more time to solve than others.

Questions 1 to 6

In the following six questions select the word in brackets which is most opposite in meaning to the word in capitals.

1. BORE (improve, engross, initiate, embrace, proclaim)

2. CATHOLIC (limited, agnostic, heathen, general, bigoted)

3. UNITY (defeat, anger, decline, strife, distrust)

4. OFFSPRING (stranger, brother, enemy, adult, ancestor)

5. ERUDITE (accurate, ignorant, regular, foolhardy, recumbent)

6. SPURIOUS (bedraggled, authentic, likely, fine, stiff)

Question 7

7. Below are seven antonyms of the keyword SHODDY. Take one letter in turn from each of the antonyms to spell out a further antonym of the word SHODDY. All letters appear in the correct order.

meticulous, considerate, accurate, fine, fastidious, superlative, excellent

Questions 8 to 13

In the following six questions, from the six words given identify the two words that you believe to be most opposite in meaning.

8. light, stolid, fluid, emotional, worried, slim

9. indecency, doubt, propriety, inaccuracy, rudeness, worry

10. animation, zip, nerve, button, devotion, lethargy

11. worth, harmony, trivia, trumpery, essentials, serenity

12. spin, rectitude, corruption, retaliation, release, gossip

13. upend, destroy, downgrade, change, ameliorate, plunge

Questions 14 to 20

The following are a miscellaneous selection of question types where, in each case, you have to identify two words with opposite meanings. Read the instructions to each question carefully.

14. MOON JAR RIM is an anagram of which two words (5, 5) that are opposite in meaning?

15. INNOCENT DREAM is an anagram of which two words (7, 6) that are opposite in meaning?

16. Complete the two words, one in each circle and both reading clockwise, which are opposite in meaning. You have to find the starting point and provide the missing letters.

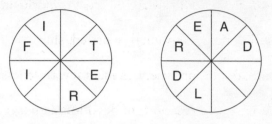

17. Complete the two words, one in each circle and both reading anti-clockwise, which are opposite in meaning. You have to find the starting point and provide the missing letters.

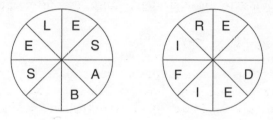

18. Complete the two words, one in each circle, one reading clockwise and the other anti-clockwise, which are opposite in meaning. You have to find the starting point and provide the missing letters, and work out which word is clockwise and which is anti-clockwise.

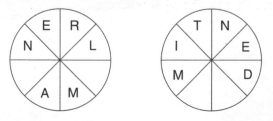

19. Each square contains the letters of a nine-letter word. Find the two words, one in each square, that are opposite in meaning.

O	A	L		
A	U	G		
S	O	N	I	F
		R	E	D
		T	F	E

20. The circles contain the letters of two eight-letter words which can be found reading clockwise. Find the two words, which are opposite in meaning. Each word starts in a different circle, and all letters appear in the correct order and are used once each only.

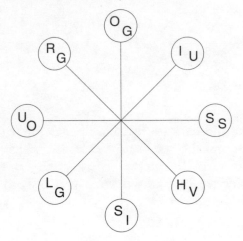

Answers to Test 2

1. engross
2. limited
3. strife
4. ancestor
5. ignorant
6. authentic
7. careful
8. stolid, emotional
9. indecency, propriety
10. zip, lethargy
11. trivia, essentials
12. rectitude, corruption
13. downgrade, ameliorate
14. major, minor
15. ancient, modern
16. terrific, dreadful
17. baseless, verified
18. mannerly, impudent
19. analogous, different
20. sluggish, vigorous

Assessment

Each correct answer scores one point.

8–10	Average
11–13	Good
14–16	Very good
17–20	Exceptional

Test 3: Analogy test

An analogy is a similitude of relations, where it is necessary to reason the answer from a parallel case. The verbal analogy test that follows is a series of 20 questions designed to test your ability to visualize relationships between various objects and ideas. You have 20 minutes in which to complete the 20 questions.

Example

TIRED is to WORK as HAPPY is to (sleep, rest, success, exercise, eating)

Answer: success. Explanation: success has a similar relationship to HAPPY as work has to TIRED because being tired could be as a result of work. From the five options given, being happy is the one most likely to be the result of success.

1. HALLMARK is to GOLD as WATERMARK is to (book, identification, ship, paper, feature)

2. RANGE is to STOVE as KILN is to (pottery, furnace, burning, heat, bake)

3. STIFLE is to SUPPRESS as FRUSTRATE is to (preclude, veto, curb, debar, censor)

4. CAESAR is to ROME as MIKADO is to (China, operetta, Asia, Japan, emperor)

5. ASPIRATION is to STRIVE as FRUITION is to (wish, realize, éclat, acknowledge, ambition)

6. BINAURAL is to EARS as BINOCULAR is to (vision, eyes, magnify, focus, twin)

7. CHOWDER is to FISH as GAZPACHO is to (vegetable, chicken, pasta, consommé, chilled)

8. KILO- is to THOUSAND as HECTO- is to (million, ten, tenth, hundred, thousandth)

9. VIXEN is to FOX as HIND is to (horse, deer, otter, zebra, rabbit)

10. SCOWL is to FROWN as HARANGUE is to (pester, wrath, temper, point, attack)

11. TACHOMETER is to DISTANCE as STEELYARD is to (hardness, weight, strength, rainfall, height)

12. CASTLE is to DEFENCE as THEATRE is to (audience, performance, arena, actor, entertainment)

13. EVENING is to NIGHT as SPRING is to (winter, season, day, summer, autumn)

14. EXPANSE is to GULF as REACH is to (sea, river, stretch, water, land)

15. VICENARY is to TWENTY as DUODENARY is to (twelve, two, forty, two hundred, two thousand)

16. DEMURE is to MODEST as DEMUR is to (defect, object, mock, postpone, charge)

17. VIADUCT is to VALLEY as CAUSEWAY is to (passage, overpass, water, railway, incline)

18. HAEMATITE is to IRON as GALENA is to (copper, tin, zinc, titanium, lead)

19. PIAZZA is to ITALY as PLAZA is to (France, Latin America, South America, Spain, Portugal)

20. SKULL is to HEAD as TALUS is to (heel, wrist, ankle, elbow, hip)

Answers to Test 3

1. paper (hallmark is a mark in gold and watermark is a mark in paper)
2. furnace (a range is a stove and a kiln is a furnace)
3. curb (to suppress is to stifle and to curb is to frustrate)
4. Japan (a Caesar was a ruler in Rome and a Mikado a ruler in Japan)
5. realize (to strive is to fulfil an aspiration and to realize is to bring something to fruition)
6. eyes (binaural relates to the ears and binocular relates to the eyes)
7. vegetable (chowder is a soup made from fish and gazpacho is a soup made from vegetables)
8. hundred (the prefix kilo- means thousand and the prefix hecto- means hundred)
9. deer (a vixen is a female fox and a hind is a female deer)
10. pester (a scowl is made by frowning and harangue is made by pestering)
11. weight (a tachometer measures distance and a steelyard measures weight)
12. entertainment (a castle is built for defence and a theatre is built for entertainment)
13. summer (evening immediately precedes night and spring immediately precedes summer)
14. river (a gulf is an expanse of water and a reach is a stretch of river)
15. twelve (vicenary refers to twenty and duodenary refers to twelve)
16. object (demure means modest and demur means object)
17. water (a viaduct crosses a valley and a causeway crosses water)
18. lead (haematite is an ore of iron and galena is an ore of lead)
19. Spain (a piazza is a square in Italy and a plaza is a square in Spain)
20. ankle (the skull is contained in the head and the talus is the ankle bone)

Assessment:

Each correct answer scores one point.

8–10   Average
11–13   Good
14–16   Very good
17–20   Exceptional

Test 4: Verbal eclectic test

Test 4 consists of a miscellaneous selection of 25 verbal questions designed to test your quickness of thought and your ability to adapt to different types of question. You have 60 minutes in which to answer the 25 questions.

1. Which of the following is not an anagram of an animal?

    leg zeal

    trap hen

    ship can

    go anorak

    fab foul

2. Which is the odd one out?

    prairie, sierra, savannah, pampas, veldt

3. Which is the odd one out?

    modify, align, regulate, remedy, adjust

4. Which is the odd one out?

    azure, cyan, indigo, emerald, sapphire

5. Which is the odd one out?

    coolabah, platypus, dingo, bandicoot, wombat

6. Which word can go after each of the groups of letters below to produce four separate words?

   FU

   BA   ***

   CAN

   PRO

7. Change one letter only in each word below to produce a familiar phrase.

   cat town so site

8. Insert the name of an artefact with musical connections into the bottom line in order to produce nine three-letter words reading downwards.

D	F	C	M	T	C	D	R	S
I	E	A	A	O	A	U	A	E
*	*	*	*	*	*	*	*	*

9. TRAGIC HORSES is an anagram of which familiar phrase (4, 2, 6)? Clue: success story.

10. Start at one of the corner letters and spiral clockwise round the perimeter, finishing at the centre square, to spell out a nine-letter word. You must provide the missing letters.

T		E
A	L	
	A	R

11. Find the starting point and work from letter to adjacent letter horizontally and vertically, but not diagonally, to spell out a 12-letter word. You must provide the missing letters.

T	N		P
A	E	E	E
L		I	R

12. Insert two letters in each set of brackets so that they finish the word on the left and start the word on the right. The correct letters should spell out an eight-letter word when read downwards in pairs.

TA (**) CK

MA (**) SK

NE (**) AR

ME (**) AS

13. Complete the six-letter words so that the last two letters of the first word are the first two letters of the second word, the last two letters of the second word are the first two letters of the third word, and so on. The last two letters of the fifth word should also be the first two letters of the first word.

** DE **

** ER **

** NI **

** LU **

** TI **

14. Insert a four-letter word into the brackets so that it completes a word when tacked onto the word on the left and completes another word when placed in front of the word on the right.

    DISC (****) COME

15. Which pair of rhyming words means sagacious moles?

16. Only one group of five letters below is an anagram of a five-letter word in the English language. Find the word.

    HUNEC

    LONRI

    MECYI

    ABICT

    TAPOD

    ANULD

    FILPO

17. What word is missing from the brackets that means the same as both definitions either side of the brackets?

    catalogue (   ) lean over

18. What two words that sound alike, but are spelt differently, mean lever up/bounty?

19. Insert the letters of the phrase ROMAN GRINNED into the blank spaces in the grid to produce a type of fruit.

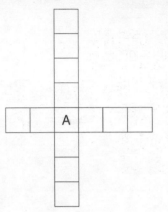

20. Add one letter, not necessarily the same letter, to the middle, beginning or end of these words to find four words on the same theme.

    seen, on, our, tree

21. Insert the letters of the phrase ABBREVIATE COIN OUTRAGE once each only into the blank spaces to find three words that are all similar in meaning.

    CS   *E****L*N*   *H******L*

22. If meat in a river (3 in 6) is T(HAM)ES, can you find a metamorphosis in a holy messenger of the highest rank (6 in 9)?

23. Add three consecutive letters of the alphabet into the group of letters below, without splitting the consecutive letters, to form another word.

    CAY

24. What is a legation?

    a.   slow passage of music

    b.   a horizontal pole on scaffolding

    c.   a diplomatic mission

    d.   a wound or injury

    e.   a narrow passage

25. What is the longest word in the English language that can be produced from the following 10 letters?

ANTIPLJUWM

Answers to Test 4

1. spinach = ship can. The animals are gazelle = leg zeal, panther = trap hen, kangaroo = go anorak, buffalo = fab foul.
2. sierra (it is a mountain chain, the rest being grassland)
3. remedy (it means to put things right or correct; the rest mean to adjust)
4. emerald (it is green, the rest being blue)
5. coolabah (it is a tree, the rest being animals)
6. TON: futon, baton, canton, proton
7. cut down to size
8. metronome
9. rags to riches
10. cathedral
11. experimental
12. pedestal: tape/peck, made/desk, nest/star, meal/alas
13. redeem, emerge, genial, allure, retire
14. OVER: discover/overcome
15. wise spies
16. TAPOD = adopt
17. list
18. prise/prize
19. mandarin orange
20. seven, one, four, three
21. gracious, benevolent, charitable
22. ar(change)l
23. canopy
24. c. a diplomatic mission
25. platinum

Assessment

Each correct answer scores one point.

8–10   Average
11–13   Above average
14–16   Good
17–20   Very good
21–25   Exceptional

Culture-fair intelligence tests

Although mastery of words is seen by many as the true measure of intelligence, there is also a belief that diagrammatic ability, shown by spatial tests, is more important than word knowledge. The definition of 'spatial' is pertaining to space, and spatial abilities mean the perceptual and cognitive abilities that enable a person to deal with spatial relations.

Advocates of such non-verbal tests argue that they examine raw intelligence without the influence of prior knowledge. Such tests are referred to as culture-fair tests, or culture-free tests, and are designed to be free of any particular cultural bias, so that no advantage is derived by individuals of one culture relative to those of another. In other words, they eliminate language factors or other skills that may be closely tied to another culture.

The tests in this chapter are all culture-fair and rely totally on diagrammatical representation. They are designed not just to test your powers of logic and your ability to deal with problems in a structured and analytical way, but to also make you think laterally and creatively.

Test 1: Spatial appreciation A

This test consists of 10 questions to test your spatial appreciation. As there are several different types of question within the test, it is necessary to read the instructions to each question first before attempting it. You have 30 minutes in which to attempt the 10 questions.

1.

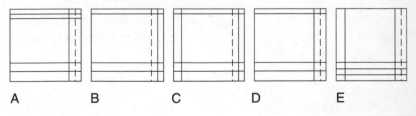

Which is the missing tile?

A   B   C   D   E

2.

Which shield below has most in common with the shield above?

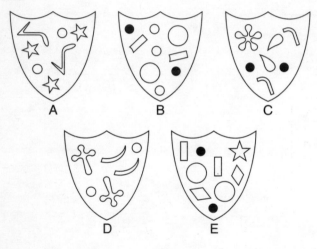

3.

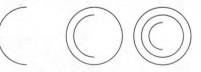

What comes next?

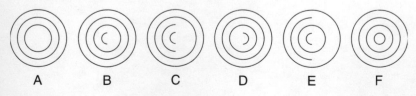

4.

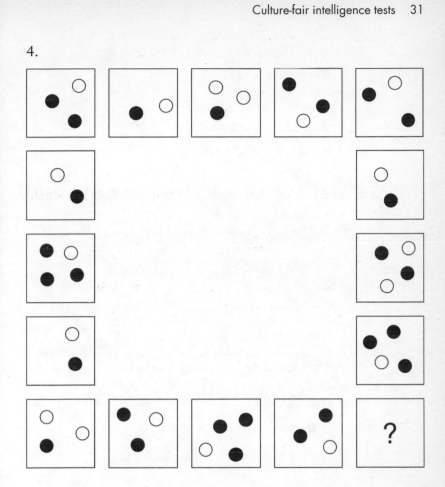

Which square should replace the question mark?

A   B   C   D   E

5.

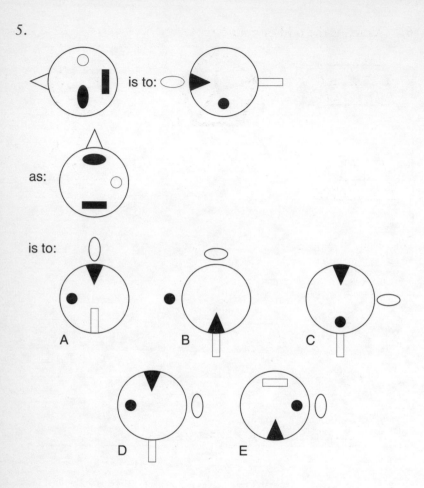

6. Which is the odd one out?

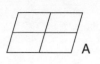
A

B

C

D

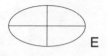
E

F

7.

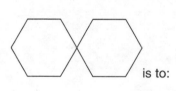

is to:

as:

is to:

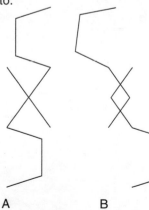

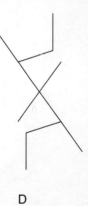

A   B   C   D

8.

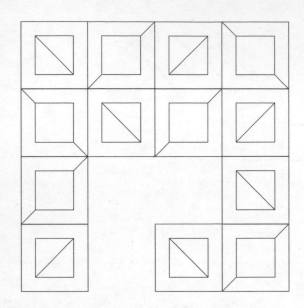

Which is the missing section?

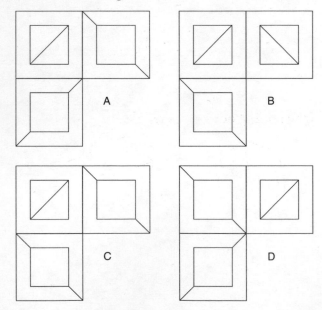

9.

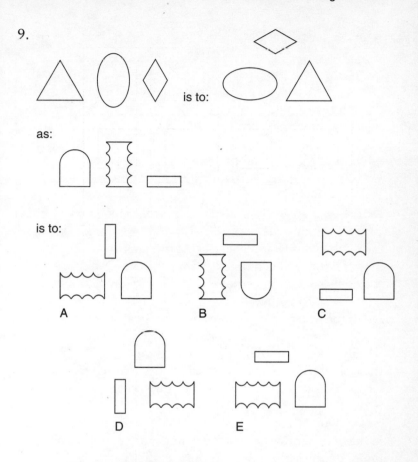

is to:

as:

is to:

A   B   C

D   E

10.   Which is the odd one out?

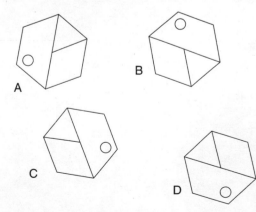

A

B

C

D

Answers to Test 1

1. D: to complete the pattern of complete and dotted lines.
2. D: the only one which contains two each of each symbol, as does the example.
3. B: circles are being built up half a circle at a time, and at each new stage the left-hand half of a new inner circle is added and the existing half circle is completed.
4. B: so that each side of five squares contains six white dots and eight black dots.
5. D: the triangle moves inside the circle and changes from white to black, the ellipse moves 90° clockwise, goes outside the circle and changes from black to white, the dot moves 180° and changes from white to black, and the rectangle rotates 90°, moves outside the circle and changes from black to white.
6. D: all the others are divided into identical segments.
7. A: the lines forming a cross in the centre do not move. The remaining lines attach themselves to the top of the cross, at the right and left corners respectively, as in the example.
8. C: so that one of each of the four different squares appears in each row and column.
9. A: the figure on the left moves to the bottom right, the figure in the middle moves to the bottom left after rotating 90°, the figure on the right moves to the top after rotating 90°.
10. C: the others are all the same figure.

Assessment

Each correct answer scores one point.

4–5   Average
6–7   Good
8   Very good
9–10   Exceptional

Test 2: Spatial appreciation B

This test also consists of 10 questions to test your spatial appreciation. As there are several different types of question within the test it is necessary to read the instructions to each question first before attempting it. You have 30 minutes in which to attempt the 10 questions.

1.

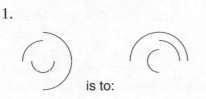 is to:

as:

is to:

A   B   C   D   E

2. Which is the odd one out?

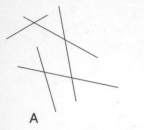 A

 B

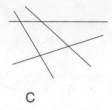 C

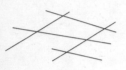 D

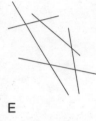 E

 F

3.

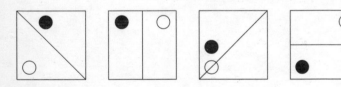

What comes next?

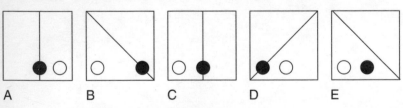

A   B   C   D   E

4.   Which is the odd one out?

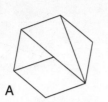

A

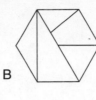

B

C

D

E

F

G

5.

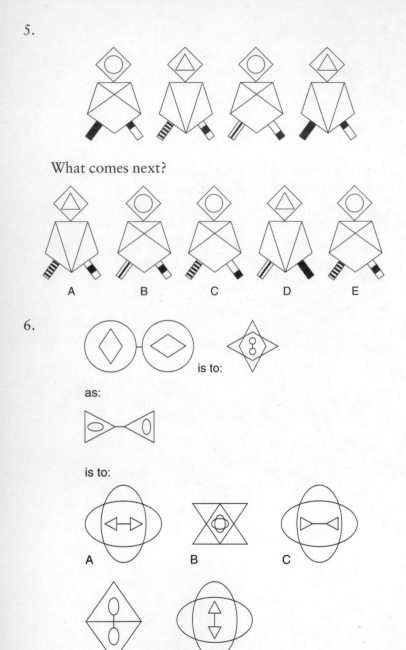

What comes next?

A   B   C   D   E

6.

is to:

as:

is to:

A   B   C

D   E

7.

To which shield below can a dot be added so that it meets the same conditions as in the shield above?

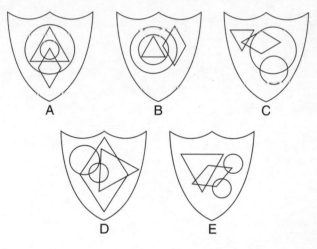

8.

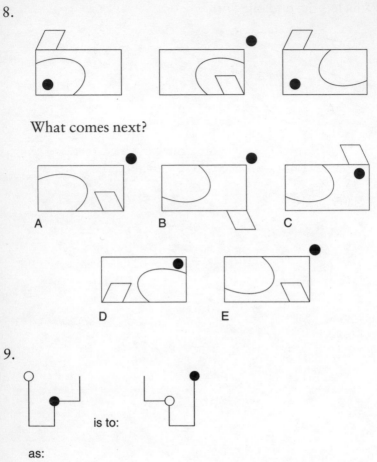

What comes next?

9.

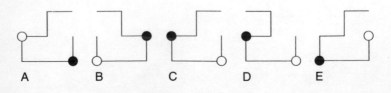

10. Which is the odd one out?

A

B

C

D

E

Answers to Test 2

1. B: The largest arc moves 90° anti-clockwise, the next largest moves 90° clockwise and the smallest arc also moves 90° clockwise
2. C: it only contains four lines. The rest contain five lines each.
3. E: the line is moving clockwise to corner/side/corner, the white dot switches between opposite corners and the black dot moves anti-clockwise side/corner/side.
4. C: A is the same as E, B is the same as F and D is the same as G.
5. E: looking across, the head repeats circle/triangle, the body repeats cross/V, the left leg repeats black/stripes/line and the right leg repeats black at top/middle/bottom.
6. F: The figures in the middle (the ellipses) increase in size and merge. The main figure (the triangles joined by a line) reduces in size, rotates 90° and goes inside the merged ellipses.
7. A: so that the dot appears in one of the circles only plus the triangle.
8. E: the parallelogram alternates between two positions, as does the black dot. The arc moves from corner to corner anti-clockwise.
9. C: the whole figure becomes a mirror image of its former self, except that the two dots change places.
10. B: all the others are a string of white/white/black/white/black/white dots.

Assessment

Each correct answer scores one point.

4–5	Average
6–7	Good
8	Very good
9–10	Exceptional

Numerical calculation and logic

As well as diagrammatic tests, numerical tests are regarded as being culture-fair to a great extent, as numbers are international. In addition to testing your powers of calculation, many of the tests in this chapter also test your powers of logic, and your ability to deal with problems in a structured and analytical way.

We all require some numerical skills in our lives, whether it is to calculate our weekly shopping bill or to budget how to use our monthly income. Anyone who has ever taken an IQ test will be familiar with the types of numerical tests encountered, and the flexibility of thought and often lateral thinking processes needed to solve them. The more one practises on these types of little puzzles, the more proficient one becomes at solving them.

Test 1: Calculation and logic A

This test is a battery of 15 number puzzles designed to test your numerical ability. You have 60 minutes in which to solve the 15 puzzles. The use of a calculator is permitted in this test.

1. What number should replace the question mark to continue the sequence?

    1, 5, 13, 29, ?

2. How many minutes is it before 12 noon if 40 minutes ago it was four times as many minutes past 10 am?

3. What number should replace the question mark?

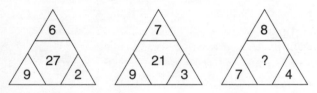

4. What number should replace the question mark to continue the sequence?

    100, 96.5, 92, 86.5, ?

5. What value of weight should be placed on the scales to balance?

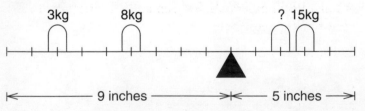

6. Tony and Cherie share a certain sum of money in the ratio 2 : 5. If Cherie has £195.00, how much money is shared?

7. Insert the numbers 1, 2, 3 , 4, 5 into the circles, one per circle, so that:

the sum of the numbers 2 and 1, and all the numbers in between total 7

the sum of the numbers 2 and 3, and all the numbers in between total 10

the sum of the numbers 5 and 3, and all the number in between total 15

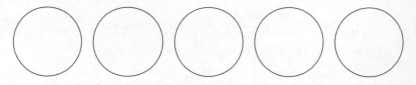

8. What is the difference between the sum (added together) of the largest two odd numbers in grid A and the product (multiplied together) of the smallest two even numbers in grid B?

A

17	14	9	5
11	24	19	18
12	13	10	7
23	28	15	16

5	20	7	18
22	32	24	4
26	14	23	36
9	21	16	15

B

9. What two numbers should replace the question marks to continue the sequence?

1, 10, 2.75, 8.25, 4.5, 6.5, 6.25, ?, ?

10. If Peter's age + Paul's age = 39
and Peter's age + Mary's age = 44
and Paul's age + Mary's age = 47
how old are Peter, Paul and Mary?

11. What numbers should replace the question marks?

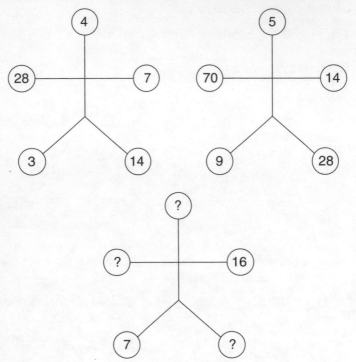

12. What is 3/11 divided by 18/44 to the smallest fraction?

13. What number should replace the question mark?

2	7	10	15
5	10	13	18
10	15	?	23
13	18	21	26

14. What number should replace the question mark to continue the sequence?

17, 34, 51, 68, ?, 102

15. What number should replace the question mark?

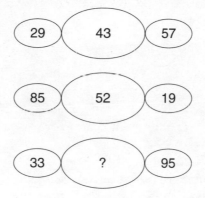

Answers to Test 1

1. 61: add 4, 8, 16, 32.
2. 16 minutes: 12 noon less 16 minutes = 11.44. 11.44 less 40 minutes = 11.04. 11.04 less 64 minutes (4 × 16) = 10 am.
3. 14: 8 × 7 = 56; 56/4 = 14. Similarly 7 × 9 = 63; 63/3 = 21.
4. 80: less 3.5, 4.5, 5.5, 6.5.
5. 4 kg

4 × 8 = 32	3 × 15 = 45
7 × 3 = $\underline{21}$	2 × 4 = $\underline{\ 8}$
53	53

6. £273.00. Each share is 273/7 (2 + 5) = £39.00. Therefore Cherie's share is 5 × 39 = 195 and Tony's share is 2 × 39 = 78.
7. 5 2 4 1 3 or 3 1 4 2 5
8. 14: A = 19 + 23 = 42 and B = 4 × 14 = 56.
9. 4.75, 8. There are two alternate sequences, one starting at 1 and adding 1.75, and the other starting at 10 and deducting 1.75.
10. Peter 18, Paul 21, Mary 26.
11. A + C = E, A × E = B, A + E + C = D.

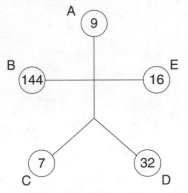

12. 2/3
    3(1)/11(1) × 44(4)/18(6) = 2/3
13. 18. Looking across each line add 5 and 3 alternately. Looking down each column add 3 and 5 alternately.
14. 85: add 17 each time.
15. 64: (33 + 95)/2. Similarly(29 + 57)/2.

Assessment

Each correct answer scores one point.

6–7   Average
8–9   Good
10–13   Very good
14–15   Exceptional.

Test 2: Calculation and logic B

This test is a further battery of 15 number puzzles designed to test your numerical ability. You have 60 minutes in which to solve the 15 puzzles. The use of a calculator is permitted in this test.

1. What number is three places away from itself plus 5, two places away from itself plus 4, three places away from itself less 3 and two places away from itself plus 2?

9	26	18	15	22
3	17	5	8	12
16	24	14	11	21
1	6	7	4	16
19	2	10	13	20

2. If a car had increased its average speed for a 150 mile journey by 5 mph, the journey would have been completed in 1 hour less. What was the original speed of the car for the journey?

3. What number should replace the question mark?

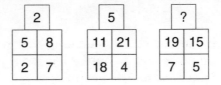

4.   What number is the odd one out?

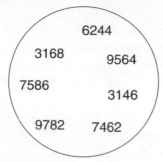

5.   What numbers should replace the question marks?

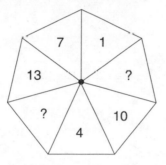

6.   What number should replace the question mark to continue the sequence?

0, 1, 2, 3, 6, 11, 20, 37, ?

7.   My watch was correct at midnight, after which it began to lose 12 minutes per hour, until 7 hours ago when it stopped completely. It now shows the time as 3.12. What now is the correct time?

8.   A golfer hits a 142 yard drive which brings his average length of drive for the round to date from 124 yards up to 126 yards. How long a drive would he have had to hit to bring his average drive for the round to date up to 131 yards?

9. What number should replace the question mark?

10. What number should replace the question mark?

1	3	1		2	3	?
2	1	2		1	4	1
1	1	1	3	1	2	2
			1	2	3	
			1	2	1	

11. A train travelling at a speed of 75 mph enters a tunnel that is 3 miles long. The length of the train is 0.25 miles. How long does it take for all of the train to pass through the tunnel from the moment the front enters to the moment the rear emerges?

12. Harry has a third as many again as Dick, who has a third as many again as Tom. Altogether they have 74. How many has each?

13. What number should replace the question mark if the answer is a whole number?

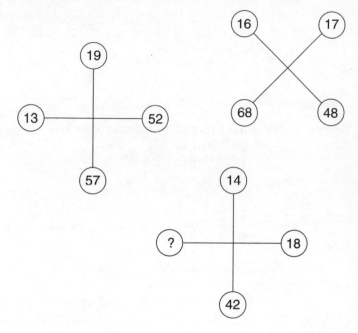

14. What two numbers should replace the question marks?

15. What number should replace the question mark?

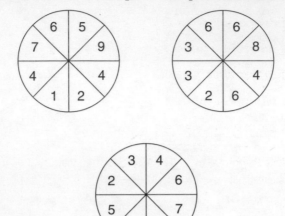

Answers to Test 2

1. 4
2. 25 mph 150/25 = 6, 150/30 = 5
3. 3: 19 + 5 = 24, 15 − 7 = 8, 24/8 = 3
4. 3146: in all the others the first and third digits multiplied together equal the number formed by the second and fourth digits. e.g. 3 × 6 = 18 (3168)
5. 16 and 19. Start at 1 and work clockwise jumping over two segments each time and adding 3.
6. 68: add the previous three numbers, i.e. 11 + 20 + 37.
7. 11 am
    12 midnight = 12 midnight
    1 am = 12.48
    2 am = 1.36
    3 am = 2.24
    4 am = 3.12
    + 7 hours = 11 am
8. 187 yards:
    8 holes × 124 average = 992 yards total
    9 holes × 126 average = 1134 yards total
    9 holes × 131 average = 1179 yards total
    992 + 187 = 1179
9. 6: 16 × 6 = 96. Similarly 35 × 2 = 70 and 29 × 3 = 87.
10. 7: the sum of the numbers in each column working left to right increases by 1 each time.
11. 2 minutes 36 seconds. 3.25 (3 + 0.25) × (60/75) = 2.6 minutes or 2 minutes 36 seconds.
12. Tom 18, Dick 24, Harry 32.
13. 72: in each set one of the smaller numbers is a third of its number opposite and the other is a quarter of its number opposite.
14. (5 + 14) × 2 = 38. (14 + 38) × 2 = 104

15. 7: two pairs of numbers opposite add up to 100, ie 23 + 77
     and 46 + 54. Similarly 36 + 64 = 100 as do 68 + 32.

Assessment

Each correct answer scores one point.

6–7   Average
8–9   Good
10–13   Very good
14–15   Exceptional

Test 3: Numerical matrix test

In all 15 questions in this test a matrix of numbers is displayed with one section missing. From the five choices presented you have to decide, by looking across each line and down each column, or at the matrix as a whole, just what pattern of numbers is occurring, and which should therefore be the missing section.

You have 45 minutes in which to complete the 15 questions. The use of a calculator is not permitted in this test, which is designed to test both your mental agility and powers of logical reasoning.

Example

1	2	3
4		6
7		9

Which of the following is the missing section?

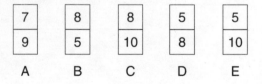

A	B	C	D	E
7 / 9	8 / 5	8 / 10	5 / 8	5 / 10

Answer: D. Explanation: The numbers 1 2 3 4 5 6 7 8 9 appear, reading across each row in turn.

1.

5	4	9
7	?	10
12	7	?

Which of the following is the missing section?

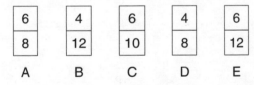

A   6   15

B   3   19

C   4   18

D   4   19

E   3   17

2.

5	2	10
3		12
15		120

Which of the following is the missing section?

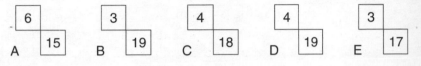

6	4	6	4	6
8	12	10	8	12
A	B	C	D	E

3.

2	4	6
5	?	9
?	10	12

Which of the following is the missing section?

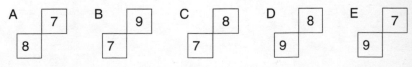

A   7   8

B   9   7

C   8   7

D   8   9

E   7   9

4.

4	3	7	10
2			20
6	12		30
8	21	29	50

Which of the following is the missing section?

9	11
	18

A

7	13
	22

B

9	11
	20

C

7	11
	18

D

9	13
	18

E

5.

24	3	8
6		2
4		4

Which of the following is the missing section?

4
2

A

4
1

B

3
1

C

3
2

D

1
3

E

6.

6	3	2	7
4	?	1	4
2	4	?	4
6	2	7	3

Which of the following is the missing section?

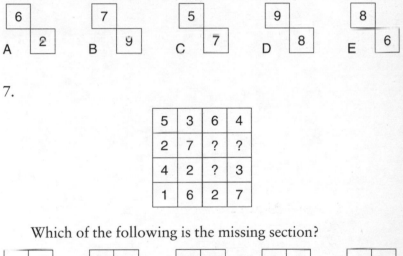

7.

5	3	6	4
2	7	?	?
4	2	?	3
1	6	2	7

Which of the following is the missing section?

8.

11	12	13	14
21	22	?	?
31	?	?	34
?	?	43	44

Which of the following is the missing section?

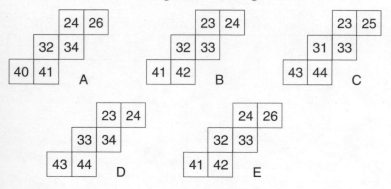

9.

4	2	3	1
6	4	5	3
5	3	?	?
7	5	?	4

Which of the following is the missing section?

2	4
6	
A

6	2
4	
B

2	1
3	
C

2	1
5	
D

4	2
6	
E

10.

3	4	2	9
6	8	5	19
?	?	1	13
?	19	8	41

Which of the following is the missing section?

5	7
14	

A

4	6
13	

B

7	5
14	

C

2	9
8	

D

6	8
8	

E

11.

14	12	10	8
17	?	13	?
20	18	?	14
23	?	19	17

Which of the following is the missing section?

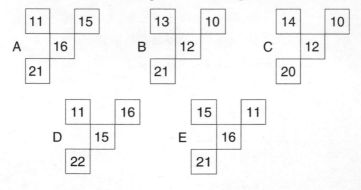

12.

5	9	7	11	9
?	?	9	13	11
3	?	5	9	7
5	?	?	11	9
1	5	3	7	5

Which of the following is the missing section?

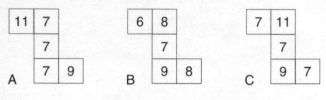

A   B   C

D

E

13.

6	7	5	8	4
3	1	2	2	1
7	8	6	9	5
2	0	1	?	?
8	9	7	?	6

Which of the following is the missing section?

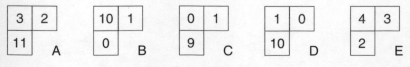

3	2
11	

A

10	1
0	

B

0	1
9	

C

1	0
10	

D

4	3
2	

E

14.

16	16	1	4	8	2
64	320	5	?	160	10
4	20	5	?	20	5
4	8	2	?	?	4
20	80	4	5	?	8
5	10	2	5	10	2

Which of the following is the missing section?

8	
16	
4	1
	20

A

16	
4	
1	4
	40

B

16	
8	
4	2
	40

C

8	
2	
4	8
	20

D

4	
1	
2	16
	30

E

15.

11	18	15	22	19	26
8	15	12	19	16	23
15	22	19	?	23	30
12	19	?	23	?	27
19	26	23	30	27	?
16	23	20	27	24	31

Which of the following is the missing section?

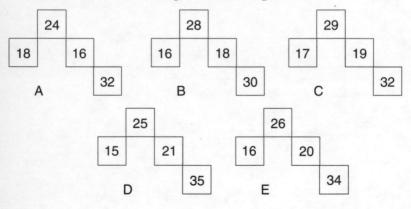

A

B

C

D

E

Answers to Test 3

1. B: in each row and column the first two numbers added together equal the third number.
2. D: in each row and column the first two numbers multiplied together equal the third number.
3. A: looking across, the numbers increase by 2; looking down, they increase by 3.
4. A: looking across and down each row and column, the first two numbers added together equal the third number and the second and third numbers equal the fourth number.
5. C: looking across and down, the middle number in each row and column is the result of dividing the third number into the first number.
6. D: each row and column totals 18.
7. B: in each row the third number is the first number plus 1, and the fourth number is the second number plus 1. Looking down each column, the respective numbers are minus 1.
8. B: looking down each column, the numbers increase by 10. Looking across each row they increase by 1.
9. E: looking across, the numbers proceed –2, +1, –2. Looking down, they proceed +2, –1, +2.
10. A: looking across and down, add the first three numbers in each row and column to obtain the final number.
11. E: looking across, the numbers reduce by 2 each time; looking down they increase by 3.
12. C: looking across, the numbers proceed +4, –2, +4, –2. Looking down, they proceed +2, –4, +2, –4.
13. D: looking across, columns 1, 3 and 5 reduce by 1 and columns 2 and 4 increase by 1. Looking down, rows 1, 3 and 5 increase by 1 and rows 2 and 4 reduce by 1.
14. B: in each set of nine corner squares every number in the middle is the product of the two numbers either side of it.
15. E: looking across, the numbers proceed +7, –3, +7, –3, +7. Looking down they proceed –3, +7, –3, +7, –3.

Assessment

Each correct answer scores one point.

6–7	Average
8–9	Good
10–13	Very good
14–15	Exceptional

Logical reasoning

How often have I said to you that when you have eliminated the impossible, whatever remains, however improbable, must be the truth.

Sir Arthur Conan Doyle, *The Sign of Four*

Logic (Greek *logos*, meaning word, speech or reason) is a science dealing with the principles of valid reasoning and argument. The classical form of argument in logical reasoning is the syllogism, which contains two premises, one major and one minor, and the conclusion that can be drawn from these two premises: For example:

All border terriers are dogs   (Major premise)
Ben is a border terrier   (Minor premise)
Therefore, Ben is a dog   (Conclusion)

A definition of logical is analytic or deductive, and this definition can be applied to someone who is capable of reasoning or using reason in an orderly, cogent fashion. The questions in this section can all be solved using this type of thinking process. There is no specialized knowledge required in order to solve them, just an ability to think clearly and analytically, and on occasions to apply some degree of lateral thinking.

Test 1: Logic test A

Test 1 consists of 20 questions of varying scope and difficulty.
You have 90 minutes in which to solve the 20 questions.

1.

387924, ? , 3724, 423, 32

What number is missing?

2.

SUNDAY

MONDAY

WEDNESDAY

SATURDAY

WEDNESDAY

MONDAY

SUNDAY

?

What comes next?

3.   Which is the odd one out?

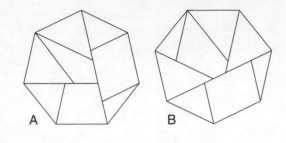

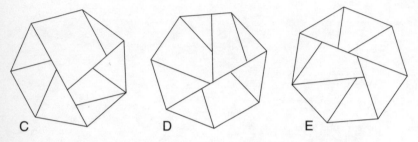

4.   Which set of letters is the odd one out?

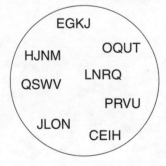

5.

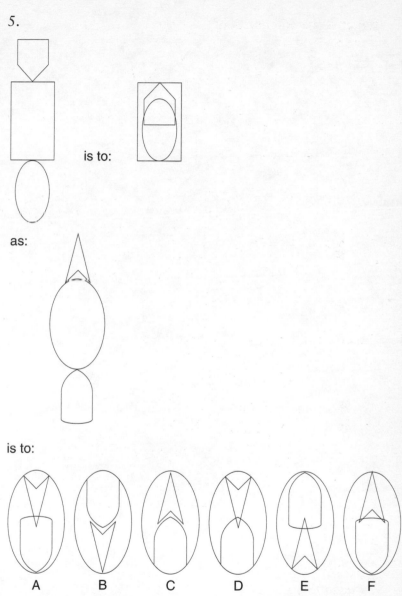

is to:

as:

is to:

A   B   C   D   E   F

6.

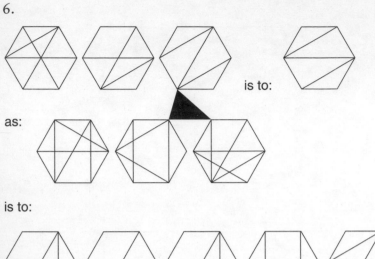

as:

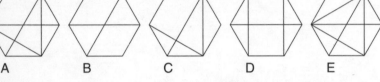

is to:

A   B   C   D   E

7.

mutiny, timely, medium

What comes next? Is it editor, fasten, endure, dismay or melody?

8.

MAT

VASE

GREEN

PAGODA

CONTEND

What comes next? Is it feather, exercise, marathon, fountain or timidity?

9.

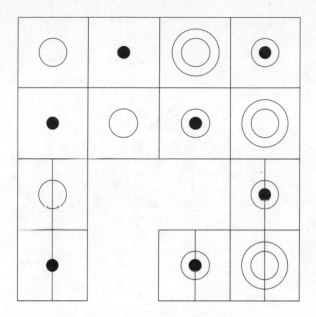

Which is the missing section?

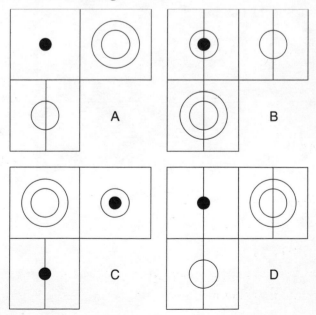

10. A car averages a speed of 30 mph over a certain distance and then returns over the same distance at an average speed of 20 mph. What is the average speed for the total journey?

11.

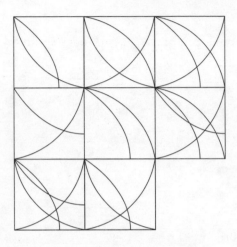

Which is the missing tile?

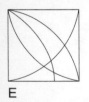

A

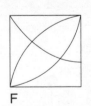

B

C

D

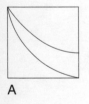

E

F

G

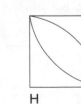

H

12. What number should replace the question mark?

3721 (8188) 5869

6257 (7695) 1842

4269 (?) 3114

13. Where would you place the numbers 4 and 6 in the grid?

7	2	9	16
13	12	3	?
?	5	14	11
10	15	8	1

14.

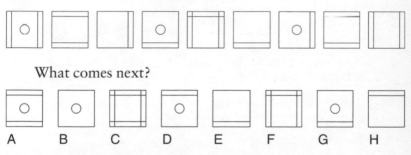

What comes next?

A   B   C   D   E   F   G   H

15. What number should replace the question mark?

		1		1		
1		2		3		
2			4	3		1
2		3			?	
	4	4				3
	3		2		3	2
1				2		

16. What four letters are missing?

K	J	P	T	M	L	K
L	M	T	P	J	K	L
M	L	K	J	P	T	M
T	P	J	?	?	M	T
P	T	M	?	?	J	P
J	K	L	M	T	P	J
K	J	P	T	M	L	K

17.

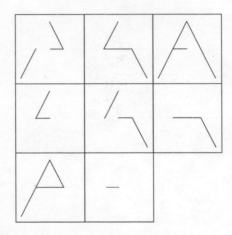

Which is the missing tile?

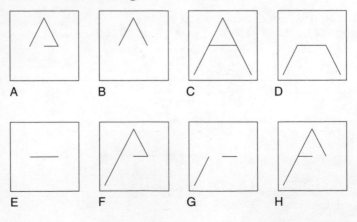

18. Three sealed boxes contain coins. The first box is labelled GOLD COINS, the second box is labelled BRASS COINS and the third is labelled GOLD OR SILVER COINS. However, all the boxes are incorrectly labelled. Which box contains which coins?

19.

384692 is to 682349

and 913746 is to 716934

therefore 482913 is to ?

20.

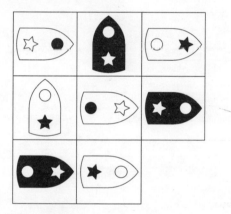

Which is the missing square?

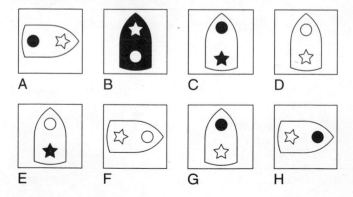

Answers to Test 1

1. 42783: reverse the previous number and discard the highest digit.
2. Sunday: an additional day is omitted each time, i.e. Sunday, Monday, (T), Wednesday, (TF), Saturday, (SMT), Wednesday, (TFSS), Monday, (TWTFS), Sunday, (MTWTFS), Sunday.
3. D: in all the others all lines start at a corner and head in the direction of another corner. D does not meet this criterion.
4. JLON: all the others are in the pattern HiJklNM, i.e. miss a letter/miss two letters and reverse the next two letters. JLON is in the pattern JkLmON.
5. A: the figures on the outside fold into the main figure.
6. A: only lines which appear twice in the first three hexagons are carried forward to the final hexagon.
7. dismay: each word starts with the middle two letters of the previous word.
8. fountain: take the last letter of each word and move two places forward in the alphabet to start the next word. The words increase in length by one letter each time.
9. D: looking across, alternate squares add a circle, and looking down, alternate squares add a line.
10. 24 mph. If the distance travelled is, say, 60 miles, then when the car averages 30 mph, the journey takes 2 hours. At 20 mph the journey takes 3 hours. This means that it takes five hours to cover 120 miles, or one hour to cover 24 miles.
11. G: looking across and down, lines are carried forward to the third square from the first two squares, unless they appear twice in the same position, in which case they are cancelled out.
12. 7175: $4 + 3 = 7$, $2 - 1 = 1$, $6 + 1 = 7$, $9 - 4 = 5$

13.

7	2	9	16
13	12	3	6
4	5	14	11
10	15	8	1

So that each horizontal, vertical and corner to corner line totals 34.

14. G: every third box has a white circle, every alternate square has a vertical right-side line, every fourth square has a vertical left line, and, starting at the second box, every alternate box has a bottom horizontal line and every third box has a top horizontal line.

15. 3: every number represents the number of times that another number is either horizontally, vertically or diagonally adjacent to it.

16.

K L
L K

Start at the bottom-left corner square and work along the bottom line, then back along the second to bottom line, etc, repeating the letters KJPTML.

17. F: looking across and down, lines are carried forward to the third square from the first two squares, unless they appear twice in the same position, in which case they are cancelled out.

18. The box labelled BRASS contains GOLD.
The box labelled GOLD or SILVER contains BRASS.
The box labelled GOLD contains SILVER.

19. 983421

A	B	C	D	E	F –	D	B	F	A	C	E
3	8	4	6	9	2 –	6	8	2	3	4	9
9	1	3	7	4	6 –	7	1	6	9	3	4
4	8	2	9	1	3 –	9	8	3	4	2	1

20. G: each row and column contains a black figure, each contains the figure pointing upwards, each contains a black dot, each contains a black star and each contains the figure with the dot and star reversed.

Assessment

Each correct answer scores one point.

8–10   Average
11–13 Good
14–16 Very good
17–20 Exceptional

Test 2: Logic test B

Test 2 also consists of 20 questions of varying scope and difficulty. You have 90 minutes in which to solve the 20 questions.

1.

NEE is to OFF

as STAR is to ?

and SHEER is to ?

What words should replace the question marks?

2.   All widgets are red. Everything red is square. Some things that are red have holes in the middle. Therefore:

a. all widgets are square.

b. everything with a hole in the middle is a widget.

c. neither of the above are true.

d. both the above are true.

3.   What word is missing from the bracket?

party (match) chime

plead (?) reefs

4.

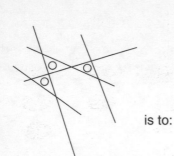   is to:

as:

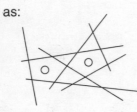

is to:

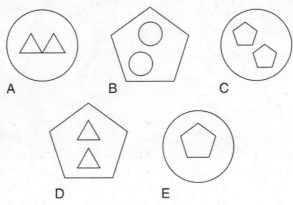

A   B   C

D   E

5.

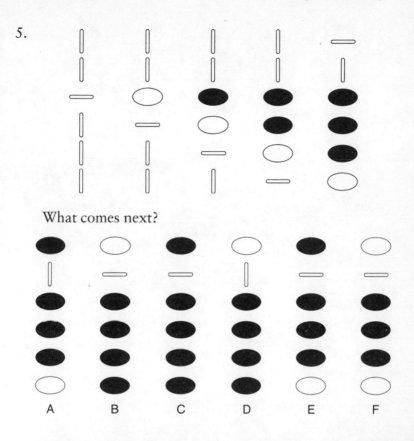

What comes next?

A   B   C   D   E   F

6. My wife usually finishes work at 4.30 pm, calls at the hypermarket, then catches the 5 pm train which arrives at our
   home town station at 5.30 pm. I leave home each day, drive
   to the station and pick up my wife at 5.30 pm, just as she gets
   off the train. One day last week my wife was able to finish
   work about 5 minutes earlier than usual, decided to go
   straight to the station instead of calling at the hypermarket,
   and managed to catch the 4.30 train, which arrived at our
   home town station at 5 pm. Because I was not there to pick
   her up she began to walk home. I left home at the usual time,
   saw my wife walking, turned round, picked her up and drove
   home, arriving there 16 minutes earlier than usual. For how
   many minutes did my wife walk before I picked her up?

7.   What number should replace the question mark?

?	5	4	2	3
1	2	3	4	3
3	2	2	1	3

8.

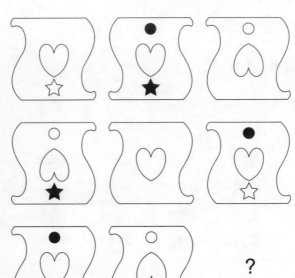

Which figure is missing?

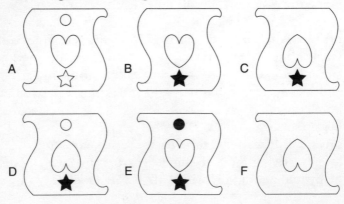

9. My thesaurus has 234 pages plus two-thirds of its total number of pages. How many pages has my thesaurus?

10.

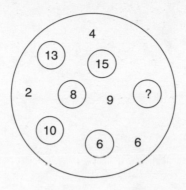

What number should replace the question mark?

11.

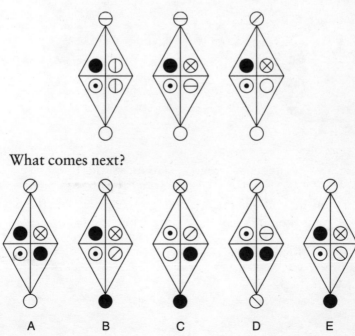

What comes next?

A   B   C   D   E

12. Which is the odd one out?

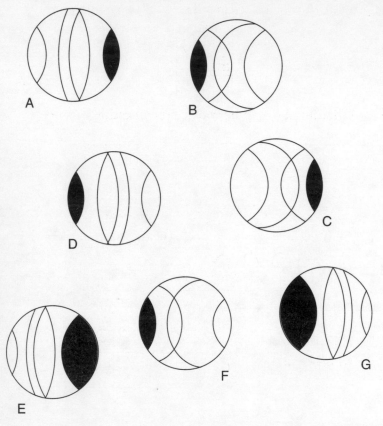

13. In a game that lasts exactly 50 minutes, there are 12 players, plus 8 reserves who alternate equally with each player. This means that all players, including reserves, are on the field of play for the same length of time. How long is that?

14.

12		11		?
	23			
		12	32	
21				

What number should replace the question mark?

15.

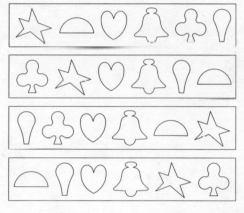

What comes next?

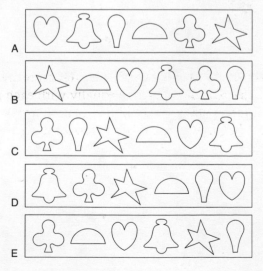

16. Jim, Sid, Alf , Jack and George took part in a golf tournament. Jack took more shots than Alf, Sid took more than Jack, Alf took more than Jim, and George took fewer than Sid. No two players took the same number of shots. Which one of the following conclusions is, therefore, proved to be correct?

a. Jack took more shots than Jim but fewer than Alf

b. Jack took fewer shots than Jim and Sid

c. Jack took more shots than Jim and Jim took fewer shots than Alf.

d. George took more shots than Alf

17.

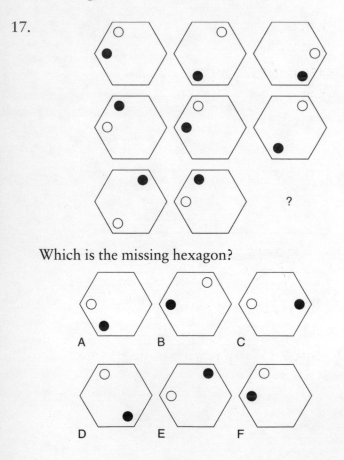

Which is the missing hexagon?

18. What percentage of the square is shaded?

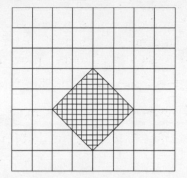

19.

    If   3618 is to 63

    and   2412 is to 42

    and   5430 is to 95

    then 4842 is to ?

20.

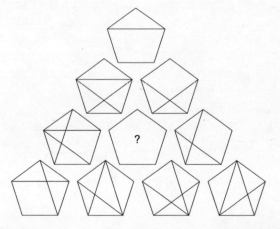

Which pentagon should replace the question mark?

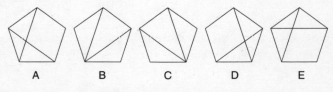

Answers to Test 2

1. STAR is to TUBS and SHEER is to TIFFS. Each letter of the first word moves one place forward in the alphabet to produce the second word.

2. a. all widgets are square

3. flare:

P A R T Y (M A T C H) C H I M E
  2   3   1 2 3 4 5   4 5   1
P L E A D (F L A R E) R E E F S

4. C: two circles enclosed in two separate pentagons become one circle enclosing two pentagons.

5. B: lines change from horizontal to vertical at each stage working downwards. At the next stage the vertical line becomes a white ellipse, and at the next stage the ellipse turns from white to black and remains black at subsequent stages.

6. 22 minutes. As I leave according to my usual schedule, we know it is before 5.30 pm when I pick up my wife. Because we have saved 16 minutes, that must be the time it takes me to drive from the point I picked her up to the station and back to the point I picked her up. Assuming it takes an equal 8 minutes each way, I have therefore picked up my wife 8 minutes before I would normally do so, which means 5.22 pm. So my wife must have walked from 5 pm to 5.22 pm, or for 22 minutes.

7. 7: starting at the top-left dot and working along the top row of dots and back along the second row, the total of the four numbers surrounding each dot reduces by 1 each time.

8. B: each row and column contains an inverted heart, a white star, a black star, a white dot and a black dot.

9. 702: 234 = 1/3; therefore, 468 = 2/3 remaining.

10. 11: add every combination in pairs of the four numbers outside the small circles to obtain the numbers inside the small circles.

11. E: every time a circle appears twice in the figure, it is replaced by two new circles at the next stage.

12. F: A is a mirror image of D, B is a mirror image of C, and E is a mirror image of G.

13. 30 minutes: $\dfrac{50 \times 12}{20}$

14. 14: each number represents the number of empty squares above it in the same column and below it in the same column.

15. B: the second figure always moves to the end, and the figure second from the end always moves to the front.

16. Statement c is correct. From the information given we know that Sid took more shots than Jack, Jack took more shots than Alf, and Alf took more shots than Jim.
    a. is incorrect because Jack took more shots than Alf.
    b. is incorrect because Jack took more shots than Jim.
    c. is correct because Jack took more shots than Alf and Jim, and Alf took more shots than Jim.
    d. is not proven because the only thing known about George is that he took fewer shots than the person who took most shots, Sid.

17. F: looking across each row, the white dot moves one corner clockwise and looking down each column it moves one corner anti-clockwise. The black dot reverses this movement.

18. 12.5% or 1/8. The square contains 8 × 8 (64) small squares, Of these, four whole squares and eight half squares are shaded, making 8 in total.

19. 87: divide the numbers formed by the first two and last two digits of the first number by 6 to arrive at the second number i.e. 48(/6)42(/6) = 87.

20. B: the contents of each pentagon are determined by the contents of the two pentagons immediately below it. Lines are carried forward from these two pentagons, except when two lines appear in the same position, in which case they are cancelled out.

Assessment

Each correct answer scores one point.

8–10   Average
11–13   Good
14–16   Very good
17–20   Exceptional

Lateral thinking

The word 'lateral' means of or relating to the side away from the median axis. Lateral thinking is a method of solving a problem by attempting to look at that problem from many angles rather than search for a direct head-on solution. It therefore involves the need to think outside the box and develop a degree of creative, innovative thinking, which seeks to change our natural and traditional perceptions, concepts and ideas. By developing this type of thinking we greatly increase our ability to solve problems that face us, that we could not otherwise solve.

To solve the questions contained in the two tests in this chapter it is necessary to think laterally and creatively and to look for solutions that may not seem apparent on first inspection.

Both tests are timed, for those of you wishing to test yourself against the clock and assess your performance. If, however, you do not wish to adopt this approach, and you just tackle the questions informally and at random, this is fine and entirely your decision. However, if this is your choice, and you do not solve any of the questions at first glance, do not necessarily rush to look up the answer, but instead return to the question later to have a fresh look. Sometimes a question that baffles you originally may suddenly appear soluble some hours or even days later.

Test 1: Lateral thinking test A

Test one consists of 10 questions of varying scope and difficulty.
You have 40 minutes in which to solve the 10 questions.

1.

  813   is to   752

  and   356   is to   231

  and   682   is to   246

  therefore   913   is to   ?

2. I bought nine apples which I carried home in four bags,
   each bag containing an odd number of apples. How is
   that possible?

3. If:

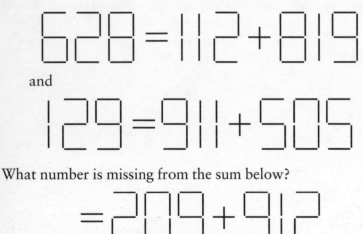

   and

What number is missing from the sum below?

4. e v e n l e i x i o n e

   The same letter is missing five times from the line of letters
   above. What letter is missing?

5.

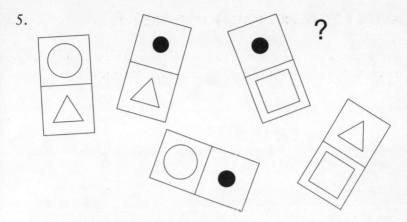

Which of the following is missing from the above group?

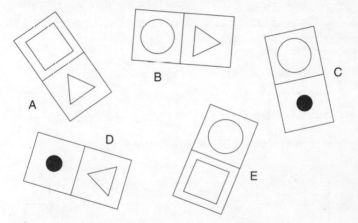

6. Grandmother is sitting in a chair, and calls her young grandson over and has him stand directly in front of her. She asks him to cup his hands in front of him and look up at the ceiling to see if he can see anything unusual, which he cannot. She then cups her hands under his, instructs him to keep his eyes on his hands and asks him to say 'Pennies from heaven'. At this point four pennies fall into his hands. Where did the pennies come from if grandmother did not have anyone assisting her in the trick?

7. 125, 150, 215, 240, 305, 330, 355, ?

    What comes next?

8. Which pair of letters are missing from this sequence?

    ia, io, ee, ae, ii, oi, ?, ee

9.

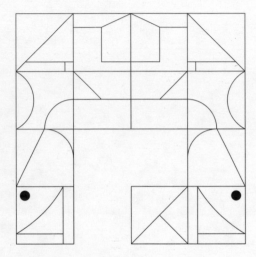

Which is the missing section?

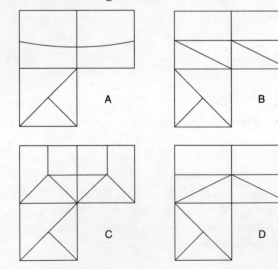

10. 272, 931, ? , 537, 394, 143

   What number is missing?

Answers to Test 1

1. 862: take the difference between the digits of the first number (913) in the following order: the difference between 9 and 1 = 8, the difference between 9 and 3 = 6, the difference between 1 and 3 = 2.
2. I put three apples each into three bags. I then put the three bags into a larger bag, which therefore contains nine apples.
3. Turn the page upside down and the calculation is correct.

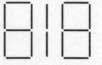

4. The letter s: seven less six is one.
5. E: to complete every possible pairing of the four different symbols, ie circle, square, triangle, black dot.
6. Grandmother has the pennies on her head.
7. 420: they are times of the day without the full point, with 25 minutes added each time; ie 1.25, 1.50, 2.15, 2.40, 3.05, 3.30, 3.55, 4.20.
8. eu: they are the vowels extracted from the question, split up into pairs.
9. D: so that the left side of the whole matrix is a mirror image of the right side.
10. 333: they are the odd numbers from 27 to 43 split up into groups of 3.

Assessment

Each correct answer scores one point.

4–5   Average
6–7   Good
8   Very good
9–10   Exceptional

Test 2: Lateral thinking test B

Test 2 also consists of 10 questions of varying scope and difficulty. You have 40 minutes in which to solve the 10 questions.

1.

A	B
formal	tacit
governor	?
elope	ruler
winch	inability

What word is missing from list B? Is it: extra, wayfarer, carriage, panic or chargehand?

2.

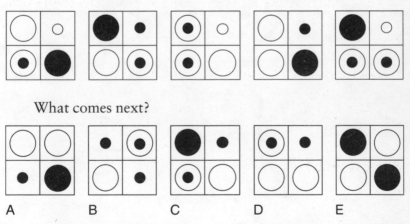

What comes next?

A   B   C   D   E

3.   The Roman numeral for 11 is XI. Add just one line to convert the Roman 11 to 6.

4. What number should replace the question mark?

5. Each morning I drive my car due north along the straight drive at the bottom of my garden, yet when I stop the car it is facing due south. How can this be so?

6. You cut a thick piece of wood into six equal pieces and stack them in two piles, each pile consisting of three pieces. You then find you have three piles of wood. Why?

7. Which is the odd one out?

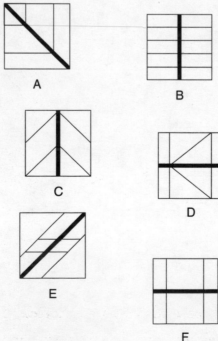

8.

If: TXE = S

FXT = T

NXT = E

TXT = S

and OXN = N

What does OXE equal?

9. Draw three complete circles, each of exactly the same size, so that each of these three circles contains one each of the three figures shown below: square, circle, triangle.

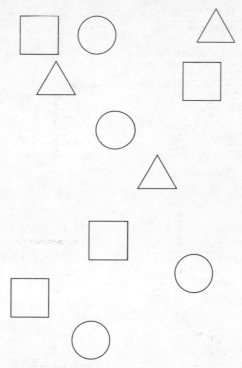

10. Why are these words in the order they are?

omega, climb, attic, speed, nurse, thief, along

Answers to Test 2

1. wayfarer. The end of the first word and the beginning of the word opposite spell out the names of countries:

    for(mal   ta)cit
    gover(nor   way)farer
    elo(pe   ru)ler
    win(ch   ina)bility

2. D: looking across, the top left-hand corner alternates white/black/white with centre dot, the top right-hand corner alternates white dot/black dot, the bottom left-hand corner alternates white with black centre dot/white and the bottom right-hand corner alternates black/white with centre dot/white.

3. Turn the XI upside-down and add the letter S to the left of the IX to produce SIX.

4. 7: looking across, the three numbers in the same segments in each pentagon total 12.

5. I am driving the car in reverse.

6. The third pile of wood is a pile of sawdust from cutting up a thick plank of wood.

7. E: in all the others the two halves separated by the thick line would be the images produced if the thick line was a mirror.

8. E: The letters stand for numbers and the X for multiplication, therefore:

    TXE = 2 × 8 = sixteen (S)
    FXT = 4 × 3 = twelve (T) or 5 × 2 = 10 (T)
    NXT = 9 × 2 = eighteen (E)
    TXT = 2 × 3 = six (S) or 3 × 2 = 6 (S)
    OXN = 1 × 9 = nine (N)
    Therefore OXE = 1 × 8 = eight (E)

9.

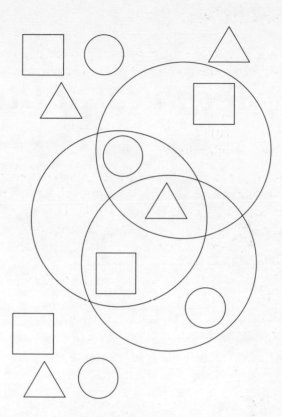

10. They end with consecutive letters of the alphabet, a, b, c, d, e, f, g.

Assessment

Each correct answer scores one point.

4–5   Average
6–7   Good
8   Very good
9–10   Exceptional

Technical aptitude

In psychology the word 'aptitude' generally means the potential for achievement. The object of aptitude testing is to determine whether a person's performance will increase markedly with additional training. Aptitude tests are, therefore, tests of performance designed to make a prediction about the future achievements of the individual being tested by measuring that individual's potential for achievement. Various types of aptitude tests can be identified, for example special and general. Special aptitude tests are designed to measure potential in a specific field such as mechanical or musical aptitude, and general aptitude tests are designed to determine potential in a wider and non-specific area. A multi-discipline intelligence test, for example, is a general aptitude test.

Technical aptitude assessment is now becoming prevalent as part of an employer's selection procedure, and often combines various disciplines such as numerical reasoning, verbal reasoning, symbolic reasoning and visual speed and accuracy, and manual dexterity tests for industry. Employees with a higher technical aptitude have the potential to master technology much more effectively and apply these skills faster than candidates with a lower technical aptitude. Employing them in technology-oriented jobs is therefore considerably more cost-effective, in terms of both training and efficiency of performance in carrying out the job at the desired level.

This requirement is particularly important, for example, with the explosion of information technology in the workplace. As new technology jobs continue to emerge, employers need to have the means at their disposal to identify candidates who will be able to learn these new technologies quickly and be able to solve complex problems in their jobs.

Test 1: Technical aptitude test A

Test 1 consists of 10 questions of a varying nature, and of varying degrees of difficulty, all designed to test your technical aptitude. You have 30 minutes in which to solve the 10 questions.

1.

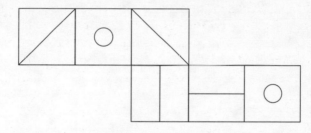

When the above is folded to form a cube, which are the only *two* of the following that can be produced?

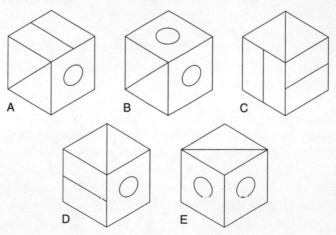

2. Which geometric figure is produced by the union of line segments AB, BC and AC?

3. You have six separate weights of 1 gm, 2 gm, 3 gm, 4 gm, 5 gm and 6 gm. Place the six weights into the empty pans so that the scales balance.

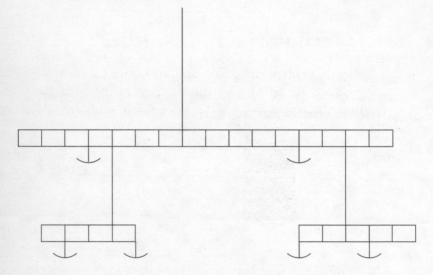

4. How many additional discs of exactly the same size as the one already placed are required to completely cover the square?

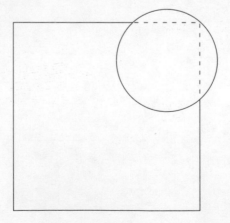

5. Where on line XY is the focal point of this double concave diverging lens?

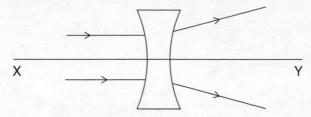

6. Two cans of identical shape and size, one black and the other silver, are filled with the same quantity of the same temperature water. Which one will cool down first?

7. How many of these items are faulty or incomplete, and why?

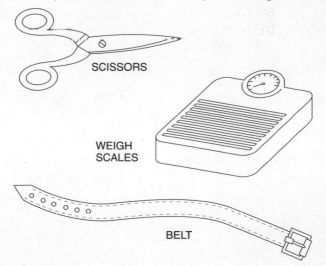

SCISSORS

WEIGH
SCALES

BELT

8.   A screw is partly inserted into a block of wood. What will happen to the screw if it is turned anti-clockwise?

9.   A wooden cube is painted blue and then cut, as shown by the dotted lines, into 27 equal cubic pieces. How many of these resultant 27 small cubes will have just two sides painted blue?

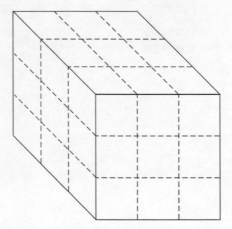

10.

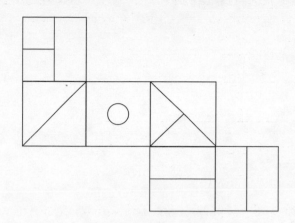

When the above is folded to form a cube, which is the only *one* of the following that can be produced?

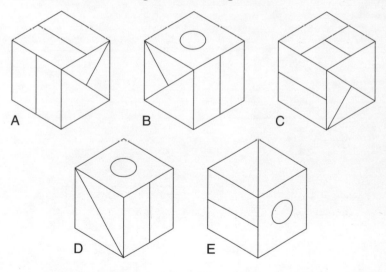

Answers to Test 1

1.   C and B
2.   a triangle

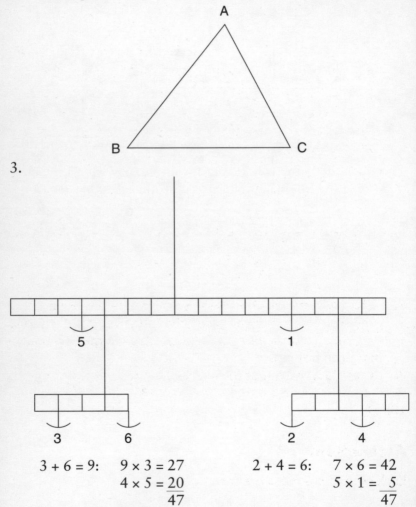

3.

3 + 6 = 9:   9 × 3 = 27
                   4 × 5 = 20
                     47

2 + 4 = 6:   7 × 6 = 42
                   5 × 1 = 5
                     47

4.   8

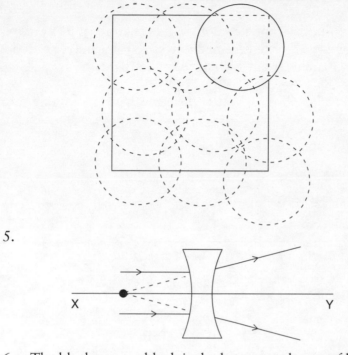

5.

6.   The black one, as black is the better conductor of heat.
7.   The scissors (the blades should be open when the handles
     are open) and the belt (there is no loop for the belt once it
     has been fastened).
8.   It would move out of the block of wood.
9.   12
10. D

Assessment

Each correct answer scores one point.

4–5	Average
6–7	Good
8	Very good
9–10	Exceptional

Test 2: Technical aptitude test B

Test 2 consists of 10 questions of a varying nature, and of varying degrees of difficulty, all designed to test your technical aptitude. You have 30 minutes in which to solve the 10 questions.

1. By what method is heat transferred from the hotplate to the water?

    a. radiation

    b. conduction

    c. thermal

    d. convection

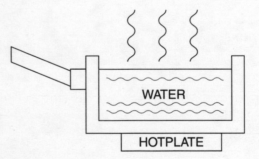

2. When pushing an object up a slope, in which direction is the load?

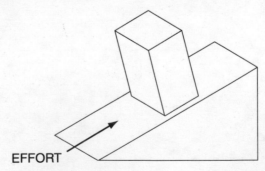

3. In the Mohs' scale of mineral hardness, talc is the softest mineral at number 1 and diamond is the hardest at number 10. In the list below, two minerals have been listed in the wrong position. Can you identify them?

    10 diamond

    9   gypsum

    8   topaz

    7   quartz

    6   orthosclose feldspar

    5   apatite

    4   fluorite

    3   calcite

    2   corundum

    1   talc

4. What colour is produced by merging yellow, cyan and magenta? Is it green, white, blue or black?

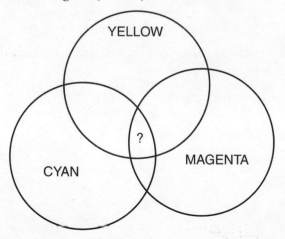

5.

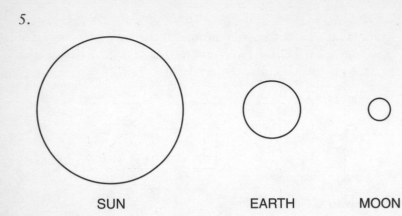

SUN   EARTH   MOON

Is this:

a. a total eclipse of the sun

b. a partial eclipse of the sun

c. a total eclipse of the moon

d. a partial eclipse of the moon

6.   When chopping a piece of wood, in which direction is the
     load?

EFFORT

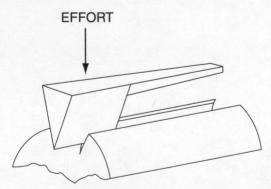

7.

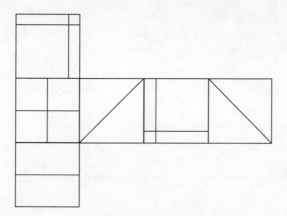

When the above is folded to form a cube, which is the only one of the following that can be produced?

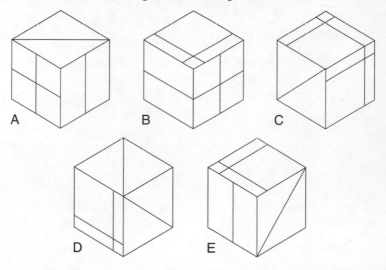

8. How many more square blocks of the same size as those already placed are required to turn this incomplete construction into a solid cube. None of the blocks already placed can be moved.

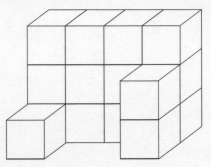

9. When both ends are pulled simultaneously how many, and which, of the following will form a knot?

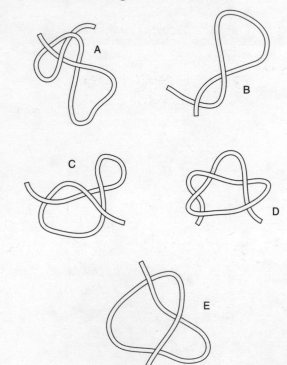

10. You have six separate weights of 1 gm, 2 gm, 3 gm, 4 gm, 5 gm and 6 gm. Place the six weights into the empty pans so that the scales balance.

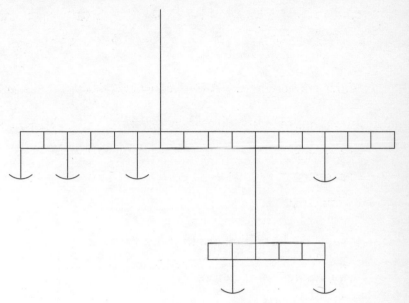

Answers to Test 2

1. b. conduction
2.

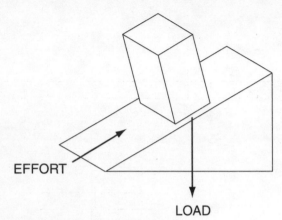

3. Gypsum and corundum are the wrong way round.
4. blue
5. c. a total eclipse of the moon
6.

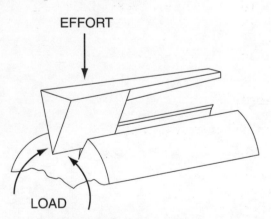

7. C
8. 49: 15 are already placed. As there are already rows of 4 at the back, the smallest cube possible is 4 × 4 × 4 (64 blocks): therefore, 49 more blocks are required.
9. A and D

10.

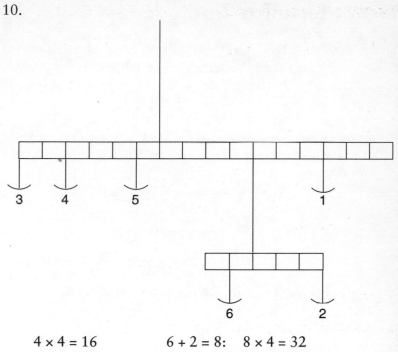

$$4 \times 4 = 16$$
$$6 \times 3 = 18$$
$$1 \times 5 = \underline{5}$$
$$39$$

$6 + 2 = 8:$ $8 \times 4 = 32$
$7 \times 1 = \underline{7}$
39

Assessment

Each correct answer scores one point.

4–5   Average
6–7   Good
8   Very good
9–10   Exceptional

Test 3: Technical aptitude test C

Test 3 consists of 10 questions of a varying nature, and of varying degrees of difficulty, all designed to test your technical aptitude. You have 30 minutes in which to solve the 10 questions.

1. How many additional discs of exactly the same size as the one already placed are required to completely cover the square?

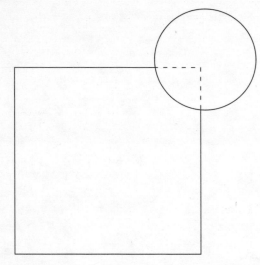

2.

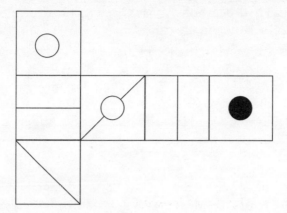

When the above is folded to form a cube, which is the only one of the following that can be produced?

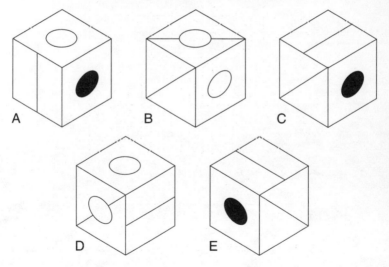

3. Symbol CH_4, can you name the simplest of the alkane or paraffin hydrocarbons? It is the main constituent of natural gas and was originally called marsh gas.

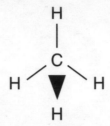

4. Which three pieces below can be fitted together to form a cuboid figure like this:

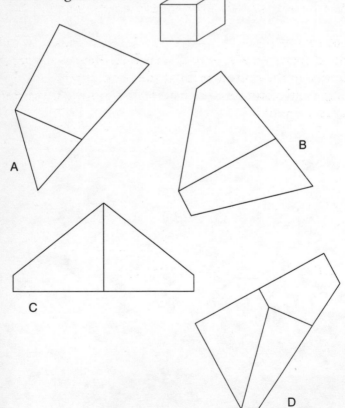

5. Where is the centre of gravity of a boomerang? Is it at A, B, C or D?

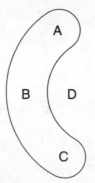

6. Which alloy is produced by combining copper and zinc?

7. The shape below is made up of seven identical cubes glued together. Six only are visible, since the seventh is hidden in the bottom right at the back. If you pick up the shape and examine it from all angles, how many different faces are visible?

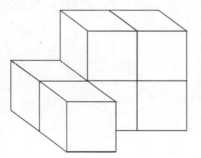

8. Which point of a compass is at 157.5°?

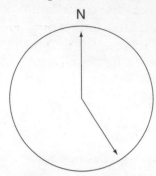

9. The following is a cross-section of which familiar device?

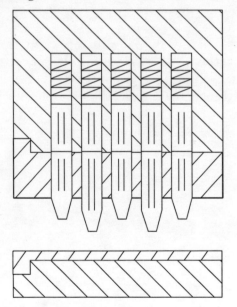

10. Two identical bottles are filled with water. The first is stored at a temperature of 40° Fahrenheit and the second at 30° Fahrenheit. They are then taken out of storage and immediately a steel ball is dropped into the neck of each bottle simultaneously. Which steel ball reaches the bottom of the bottle first?

a. the one at 40 °F

b. the one at 30 °F

c. the temperature makes no difference and they reach the bottom at the same time.

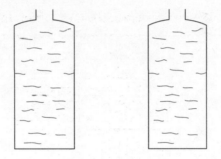

Answers to Test 3

1. 7

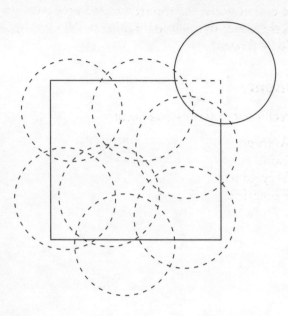

2. A
3. methane
4.

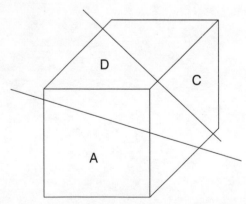

5. D: a boomerang rotates around its centre of gravity.
6. brass
7. 28

8.   south-south-east (SSE)
9.   a Yale lock
10. a. the one at 40 °F. As the freezing temperature of water is 32 °F, the water in the bottle which had been stored at 30 °F would be frozen.

Assessment

Each correct answer scores one point.

4–5   Average
6–7   Good
8   Very good
9–10   Exceptional

Mental agility

In psychology a speed test is a general term for any test that measures ability by determining the number of problems that can be dealt with successfully within a fixed time period. According to this definition, the majority of intelligence tests (IQ tests) are speed tests; indeed, one definition of intelligence is the ability to think quickly.

The ability to think quickly and under pressure, agility of mind or mental agility, is a valuable asset to have at one's disposal in many situations. The opposite to a speed test is a power test, which is defined as any test that measures ability by determining the degree of difficulty of test content that can be mastered with no time pressures on the test taker.

All the tests in this chapter are speed tests against the clock, which enable you to deal with just one question at a time while under pressure. The questions in themselves are not particularly difficult; however, when presented as a series of questions to be attempted within a set time limit, the brain must adapt to the situation before it, and mental agility plus a great deal of concentration is required in order to score highly.

The use of pencil and paper is permitted in these tests.

Test 1: Speed test A

Test 1 is a speed test of 25 questions designed to test your powers of mental calculation and logic. You have 40 minutes in which to complete the 25 questions.

1. What is twelve thousand, twelve hundred and twelve, less eleven thousand, eleven hundred and eleven?

2. If you have four-fifths of £100 and spend £36.00, how much will you be left with?

3. If the word PINT is written under the word SAFE, the word THUD is written under the word PINT and the word HOPE is written above the word safe, what word can be read diagonally?

4. If Friday is the fourth day of the month, what day is the 13th day of the month?

5. 42937816529835217643

    What is the sum of all the odd numbers that are immediately followed by an even number in the list above?

6. Harry has twice as many as Dick. Altogether they have 84. How many has each?

7. If four people all said 'hello' to each other once, how many times would the word hello be spoken?

8. Count the number of times the letter 'e' appears in this sentence. What is the total?

9. This is a mirror image of a clock face. What time was it 30 minutes ago?

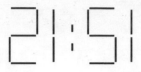

10.

Wales 2	Scotland 2
France 2	Argentina 4
Brazil 2	Ireland 3
Cameroon 4	Chile 2
England 2	Switzerland ?

How many did Switzerland score?

11. C H A R I T A B L E

Using the letters contained in the word 'charitable', once each only at a time, which is the only word of the following that cannot be produced:

calibrate, bacterial, bleach, recital, richer, eclair

12.

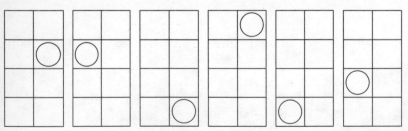

What does not belong in the above sequence?

13. What number is 30 less than when multiplied by 6 times itself?

14. Multiply half of 77 by 2 and add 46. What is the answer?

15. Which is greater, 1/3 or 2/5?

16. Which figure is wrong in this list?

17. Which number between 1 and 36 appears twice in the grid, and which number between 1 and 36 is missing?

24	10	13	6	8	21
34	15	30	17	14	3
4	25	1	35	31	29
16	20	18	26	11	22
7	36	9	2	16	32
12	33	19	23	27	5

18.

V	N	V	W	E	V	E
M	E	W	F	F	N	V
W	N	E	M	W	F	M
F	E	M	V	E	W	V
F	N	W	M	F	M	E
N	V	M	N	V	F	W
W	N	M	F	N	E	N

Which is the only letter to appear nine times in the above grid?

19.

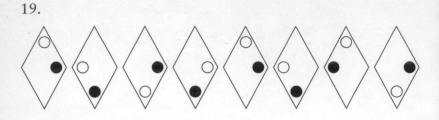

Which is wrong in the above sequence?

20. Put these words in alphabetical order:

earthquake

easterlies

earthiness

eastertide

easterners

earwigging

earthliest

21. Which three of these numbers add up to 50?

11, 13, 15, 18, 19, 23

22. If I walk 2 miles east, then 4 miles south, then 3 miles east, then 4 miles north, then 2 miles west; how far away and in what direction will I be from my starting point?

23.

AB

ABD

ABDG

ABDGK

?

What comes next?

24. Which square does not belong in this sequence?

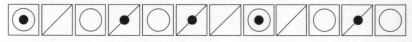

25. What is the day and date 27 days after Wednesday 11 June?

Answers to Test 1

1. 1101

    | 12000 | 11000 |
    | 1200 | 1100 |
    | 12 | 11 |
    | 13212 | 12111 |

    13212 – 12111 = 1101

2. £44.00

3. HAND

    H O P E
    S A F E
    P I N T
    T H U D

4. Sunday

5. 34:

    42937816529835217643

6. Dick 28, Harry 56

7. 12 times
    Call the people ABCD

    | AB | BA |
    | AC | CA |
    | AD | DA |
    | BC | CB |
    | BD | DB |
    | CD | DC |

    Note that: A says 'hello' to B and B says 'hello' to A, so that there are two 'hellos' in every greeting.

8. eleven

9. 11.45

   21.51 in a mirror reads as 12.15.

10. 3: the number of vowels in each country equals that country's score.

11. richer

12.

The circles moves three places anti-clockwise at each stage.

13. 6

14. 123 (77 + 46)

15. 2/5

16.

Each number is rotating 90° at each stage. The above figure should be as below:

17. 28 missing, 16 appears twice.

18. the letter N

19.

The white dot moves one corner anti-clockwise at each stage and the black dot alternates between just two positions.

20. earthiness, earthliest, earthquake, earwigging, easterlies, easterners, eastertide

21. 19 + 18 + 13

22. 3 miles east

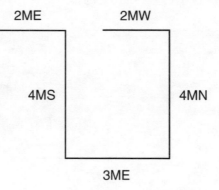

23. ABDGKP: miss an extra letter of the alphabet each time when adding the next letter, for example ABDGhijK, ABDGKlmnoP

24.

Every alternate square contains a circle, every third square contains a dot and, starting from the second square, every alternate square contains a diagonal line.

25. Tuesday 8 July.

Assessment

Each correct answer scores one point.

8–10	Average
11–13	Above average
14–16	Good
17–20	Very good
21–25	Exceptional

Test 2: Speed test B

Test 2 is a speed test of 10 questions of varying types. Some questions will take longer than others to solve, so work as quickly as possible and do not spend too much time on any one question. You have 30 minutes in which to complete the 10 questions.

1. Arrange the blocks in the correct order so that they spell out the names of three types of vehicle.

| AN | R | MO | CE | TR | USI | TO | AM | LI | AC | UL | NE | B |

2. Which five consecutive numbers add up to 27?

    68972469537294382517854 2968185

3. Find a string of five numbers in a straight line in the first grid, either horizontally, vertically or diagonally, that is repeated in the second grid either horizontally, vertically or diagonally.

4	6	5	9	7	1	6
3	8	6	2	5	2	9
5	6	9	1	3	5	2
7	4	8	5	6	8	1
2	9	7	8	5	1	3
2	4	8	1	7	9	6
6	2	9	4	3	8	1

5	6	3	9	7	2	8
4	9	7	6	3	5	2
5	8	1	3	7	9	8
6	2	7	5	3	4	1
9	6	2	3	5	7	8
4	2	6	1	8	9	5
1	4	8	3	7	5	2

4. 7462693148671932

    Multiply the number of times that an even number is followed by an odd number, by the number of times that an odd number is followed by an even number in the list above.

5. Which four-letter word that appears in the left-hand grid, also appears in the right-hand grid? The words can appear horizontally, vertically, diagonally, backwards or forwards, up or down in either grid, but always in a straight line.

T	R	I	M	E	E
U	U	A	M	I	D
T	S	A	P	F	I
T	H	A	E	R	T
S	C	A	G	E	E
K	T	S	T	E	M

A	S	K	I	S	S
C	E	F	E	A	T
N	A	N	R	M	O
I	I	S	I	E	P
P	U	S	H	N	E
S	O	H	C	E	N

6. Divide 72 by a quarter and add 3. What is the answer?

7. 8 7 4 6 9 2 8 4

    What is the difference between the average of these numbers and the second highest even number?

8. Find the starting point and trace along the connecting lines to spell out a 14-letter word.

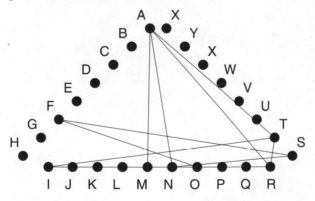

9.   3849276841937482

Delete all the numbers that appear more than once in the above list and multiply the remaining numbers together. What is the answer?

10. YPJEMDKSHFDHSJMOINWKUEDGILTYLREGINPTW

Delete all the letters that appear more than once in the above list. What are you left with?

Answers to Test 2

1. limousine, tractor, ambulance
2. 46953
3. 62357

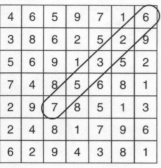

4. 6. Two even numbers and three odd.
5. feat

6. 291
7. 0: average = 6, second highest even number = 6.
8. transformation
9. 6: 6 × 1
10. FOUR

Assessment

Each correct answer scores one point.

4–5	Average
6–7	Good
8	Very good
9–10	Exceptional

Test 3: Speed test C

Test 3 is a speed test of 20 questions designed to test your powers of concentration and your ability to follow instructions. You have 20 minutes in which to complete the 20 questions.

In each of the following, arrange the letters in alphabetical order followed by the numbers in ascending numerical order. For example 2K98JA3 = AJK2389

1. S57PT4C

2. 8K5TJM47P

3. ZK9PXL428

4. 582Q7T4ES

5. 2F39YMK5P

6. J48LN3TG7M

Now arrange the letters in reverse alphabetical order, followed by the numbers in ascending numerical order.

7. S47TKQ2Y6

8. 2JM39TZ74L

9. DR3MS2975N

10. 6BF925YLK7JT

Now arrange the numbers in descending order, followed by the letters in reverse alphabetical order.

11. T4J76MQD9L

12. 7C43KMPR6SF

13. 9BK7JLS26PZV5

14. 2D3XPN75CU9T

Now arrange the vowels in forward order, followed by the numbers in reverse order, followed by the consonants in reverse order.

15. J6P928UZR4MDE

16 7EM94UJBALDF6

17. GSU75ZK8P23AT

Arrange the consonants in reverse order, followed by the even numbers in ascending order, followed by the vowels in reverse order, followed by the odd numbers in reverse order.

18. T5ULM84AZ39ER2

19. E96PTL2J75UKD8

20. 7U5E6943PSVA8L

Answers to Test 3

1. CPST457
2. JKMPT4578
3. KLPXZ2489
4. EQST24578
5. FKMPY2359
6. GJLMNT3478
7. YTSQK2467
8. ZTMLJ23479
9. SRNMD23579
10. YTLKJFB25679
11. 9764TQMLJD
12. 7643SRPMKFC
13. 97652ZVSPLKJB
14. 97532XUTPNDC
15. EU98642ZRPMJD
16. AEU9764MLJFDB
17. AU87532ZTSPKG
18. ZTRML248UEA953
19. TPLKJD268UE975
20. VSPL468UEA9753

Assessment

Each correct answer scores one point.

8–10   Average
11–13   Good
14–16   Very good
17–20   Exceptional

Test 4: Spatial test

Test 4 is a battery of 10 visual questions. You have 15 minutes in which to complete the 10 questions.

1.

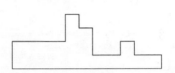

Which shape below is identical to the shape above?

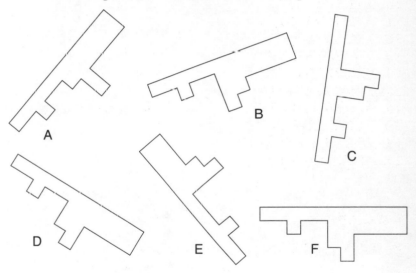

2. Which is the odd one out?

3. Which is the odd one out?

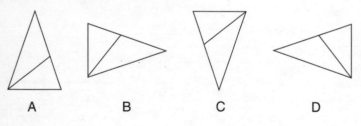

A   B   C   D

4.   How many lines appear below?

5.   Which is the odd one out?

A   B   C   D   E

6.   How many different sizes of circle are there below?

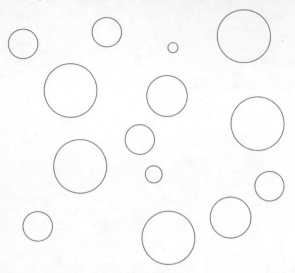

7.   Which two shapes are identical?

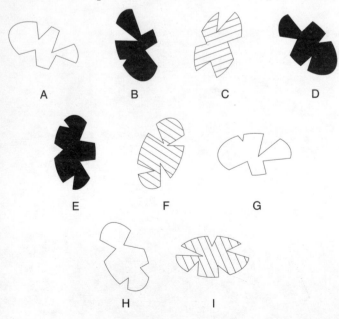

A   B   C   D

E   F   G

H   I

8. Which is the odd one out?

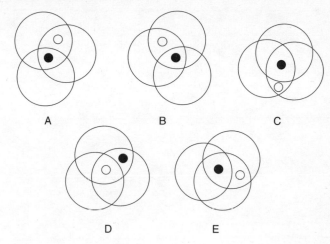

9. Which two pieces below will fit together to form a perfect square?

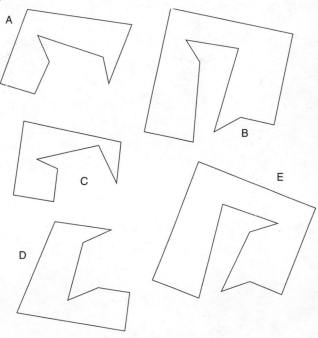

10. Which is the odd one out?

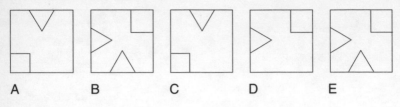

A   B   C   D   E

Answers to Test 4

1. D
2. C: all the others have an identical pairing but with black/white reversal.
3. B: the rest are the same figure.
4. 18
5. B: it has one dot in two circles and the other in three circles. The rest have one dot in one circle and the other dot in two circles.
6. 5
7. B and G
8. D: the white dot is in three circles and the black dot in two. In the others the white dot is in two circles and the black dot in three.
9.

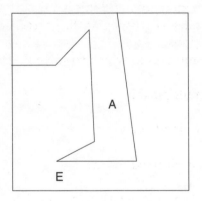

10. D: all the others have identical pairing, ie A/C and B/E.

Assessment

Each correct answer scores one point.

4–5	Average
6–7	Good
8	Very good
9–10	Exceptional

Test 5: Mental arithmetic

It is evident that mental arithmetic is not practised in today's education system to the extent that it was many years ago. Perhaps this is not completely surprising with the widespread use of calculators and computers. However, skill at mental arithmetic is still a valuable asset to have at one's disposal, and it is also an excellent way of exercising the brain and keeping your mind alert.

The following is a mental arithmetic speed test of 30 questions which gradually increase in difficulty as the test progresses. Only the answer must be committed to paper, and, of course, the use of calculators is not permitted.

You should work quickly and calmly and try to think at all times of the quickest and most efficient way of solving the questions. As well as agility of mind this is a test of your ingenuity, as there are short cuts to arriving at the correct solution for many of these calculations.

You have 45 minutes in which to solve the 30 questions.

1. What is 7 multiplied by 6?

2. What is 148 divided by 4?

3. What is 11 multiplied by 15?

4. What is 60% expressed as the lowest fraction?

5. Multiply 9 by 8 and divide by 3.

6. Divide 84 by 7 and add 17.

7. What is 15% of 150 multiplied by 2?

8. What is 7/8 of 168?

9.   What is 4/5 of 125 plus 19?

10. Multiply 9 by 7 by 4.

11. Divide 126 by 9 and add 34 multiplied by 2.

12. Multiply 58 by 21.

13. What is 7 multiplied by 5 multiplied by 3?

14. What is 40% of 140 multiplied by 5?

15. Add 27 + 32 + 7 + 18 + 19.

16. Multiply 8 by 22 and add 37.

17. What is 5/9 of 216?

18. Which is the greater: 80% of 340 or 30% of 900?

19. Divide 426 by 6.

20. Add 3/4 of 48 to 3/5 of 95.

21. Multiply 85 by 13.

22. What is 70% of 950?

23. Add 7562 to 9189.

24. Subtract 758 from 1325.

25. Subtract 87 from 166 and multiply by 3.

26. Multiply 89 by 11.

27. Subtract 2/3 of 96 from 7/8 of 464.

28. Add 19 + 27 + 18 and divide by 8 + 5 + 14 + 5.

29. Divide 784 by 56.

30. Multiply 348 by 24.

Answers to Test 5

1. 42
2. 37
3. 165
4. 3/5
5. 24
6. 29
7. 45
8. 147
9. 119
10. 252
11. 82
12. 1218
13. 105
14. 280
15. 103
16. 213
17. 120
18. 80% of 340 = 272; 30% of 900 = 270
19. 71
20. 93
21. 1105
22. 665
23. 16751
24. 567
25. 237
26. 979
27. 342
28. 2
29. 14
30. 8352

Assessment

Each correct answer scores one point.

12–15	Average
16–21	Good
22–26	Very good
27–30	Exceptional

IQ tests

Intelligence quotient (IQ) is an age-related measure of intelligence level, and is defined as 100 times the mental age. The word 'quotient' means the result of dividing one quantity by another, and intelligence can be defined as mental ability or quickness of mind.

An intelligence test (IQ test) is, by definition, any test that purports to measure intelligence. Generally such tests consist of a graded series of tasks, each of which has been standardized with a large representative population of individuals. Such a procedure establishes the average IQ as 100.

IQ tests are part of what is generally referred to as psychological testing. Such test content may be addressed to almost any aspect of our intellectual or emotional make-up, including personality, attitude and intelligence. In different parts of the world a wide range of such tests is in use. These include achievement tests, which are designed to assess performance in an academic area; aptitude tests, which predict future performance in an area in which the individual is not already trained, and IQ tests.

The earliest known attempts to rank people in terms of intelligence dates back to the Chinese Mandarin system, when studying the works of Confucius enabled successful candidates to enter the public service. Great care was taken with such tests even in those days, to the extent that to guarantee fairness to every candidate an amanuensis was employed to copy out each paper, so that no one's handwriting could be recognized and no favouritism would be shown.

The top 1 per cent of candidates were successful in progressing to the next stage, where they would again be run off against each other, and the procedure repeated yet again through a final layer of selection. Thus, the chosen candidates were in the top 1 per cent of the top 1 per cent of the top 1 per cent.

The Mandarin system worked as a purely administrative system and survived a millennium. However, because it relied so much on the works of Confucius, critics argue it was essentially anti-creative in nature, in the same way that the works of Aristotle and Plato so much dominated people's minds in Europe during the Middle Ages.

The first modern intelligence test was devised in 1905 by the French psychologists Alfred Binet and Theodore Simon. The pair developed a 30-item test with the purpose of ensuring that no child be denied admittance to the Paris school system without formal examination.

In 1916 the US psychologist Lewis Terman revised the Binet–Simon scale to provide comparison standards for Americans from age three to adulthood. Born in 1877, in Johnson County, Indiana, Terman devised the term 'intelligence quotient' and developed the so-called Stanford–Binet intelligence test to measure IQ, after joining the faculty of Stanford University as professor of education. The Stanford–Binet test was further revised in 1937 and 1960, and remains today one of the most widely used of all intelligence tests.

During the 1930s controversies surrounding the definition and make-up of intelligence led to the development of the Wechsler–Bellevue scale of intelligence in the United States, which as well as measuring general mental ability, also revealed patterns of intellectual strengths and weaknesses. The Wechsler tests extend from pre-school to adult age range, and are now as prominent as the Stanford–Binet test.

It is generally believed that a person's IQ rating is hereditary, and that a person's mental age remains constant in development to about the age of 13, after which it is shown to slow up; and beyond the age of 18, little or no improvement is found.

It is further believed that the most marked increase in a person's IQ takes place in early childhood, and theories have been put forward recently about different contributory factors. For example, recent experiments in Scandinavia have suggested that increased breast feeding in babies has resulted in a higher IQ; and research in Japan has shown that the playing of computer games by children, which involve a high degree of skill and agility of mind, have also resulted in higher IQ measurement.

Because after the age of 18 little or no improvement is found, adults have to be judged on an IQ test whose average score is 100, and the results graded above and below this norm according to known test scores. A properly validated test would have to be given to several thousand people and the results correlated before it would reveal an accurate scientific measurement of a person's IQ.

When the IQ of a child is measured, the subject attempts an IQ test that has been standardized, with an average score recorded for each age group. Thus, a 10-year-old child who scored the results expected of a child of 12 would have an IQ of 120, calculated as follows:

$$\frac{\text{mental age (12)}}{\text{chronological age (10)}} \times 100 = 120 \text{ IQ}$$

Like most distributions found in nature, the distribution of IQ takes the form of a fairly regular bell curve. On the Stanford–Binet intelligence scale half of the population fall between 90 IQ and 110 IQ (half of them above and half below), 25 percent score above 110, 11 percent above 120, 3 percent above 130 and 0.6 percent above 140. Only one person in a thousand has an IQ of 150 and one in 10 000, 160. At the opposite end of the curve, the same kind of proportion occurs.

There are several different type of intelligence scale, some more widely used in different parts of the world than others, although they all produce a similar percentage distribution, and as a result, the same bell curve shape. The IQ totals in the figure below, for example, are based on the Cattell scale of intelligence.

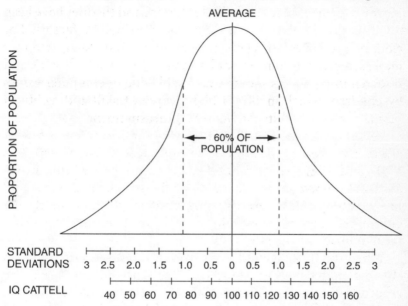

Although all test scores are generally known as intelligence quotients, or IQs, the various tests can be constructed quite differently. The Stanford–Binet is heavily weighted with items testing verbal abilities, while the Wechsler scales consist of two separate verbal and performance sub-scales, each with its own IQ. The Cattell also incorporates separate tests of verbal and spacial abilities, with separate IQ ratings.

Because IQ is hereditary, it is not possible to increase your actual IQ. However, it is possible to improve your performance on IQ tests by practising the many different types of question, and learning to recognize the recurring themes. The questions in the two tests that follow are, like many of the tests in other chapters of this book, typical of the type and style of question you are likely to encounter in actual tests, and are designed to provide valuable practice for anyone who may have to take this type of test in the future.

IQ tests are set and used on the assumption that when taking the test, you know nothing of the testing method and very little about the question methods within the tests themselves. Therefore, if you learn about this form of testing and know how to approach the different types of questions, you can improve your performance in the actual tests.

By practising on different types of IQ tests, and by getting your mind attuned to the various types of questions you may encounter, and the thought processes necessary to solve them, it is possible to improve by several vital percentage points. This may prove crucial in increasing your job prospects, and mean the difference between success and failure when you attend one of the many job interviews that include the taking of an IQ test.

The tests that follow have been newly compiled for this book, and are not standardized, so an actual IQ assessment cannot be given. However, there is a guide to assessing your performance at the end of each test, and there is also a cumulative guide for your overall performance on both tests.

It should be pointed out that intelligence tests only measure one's ability to reason. They do not measure the other qualities that are required for success, such as character, personality, talent, persistence and application. Cynics say that the only thing that having a high IQ proves is that the individual has scored well on an intelligence test; but despite some weaknesses, the IQ test remains the only known and tried method of measuring intelligence. It is crucial, however, that IQ test results be viewed as only one kind of information about an individual.

Test 1: IQ test A

Test 1 consists of a battery of 30 questions equally divided between verbal, numerical and diagrammatic disciplines. A time limit of 60 minutes is allowed for the test. Calculators may be used to assist with solving numerical questions where preferred.

1. Bill has £30.00 more than Alan, but then Alan wins some money on lotto and trebles his money, which means that he now has £20 more than the original amount of money that the two men had between them. How much money did Bill and Alan have between them before Alan's win?

2. Beauty is to aestheticism as pleasure is to: nihilism, humanism, hedonism, behaviourism, positivism

3.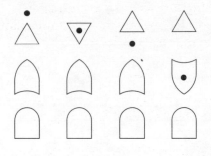

Which two options come next?

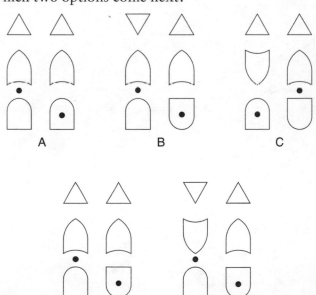

4.   100, 88, 91, 79, 82, ?

What comes next?

5.   Change one letter only in each word below to form a familiar phrase:

no dark tide

6.

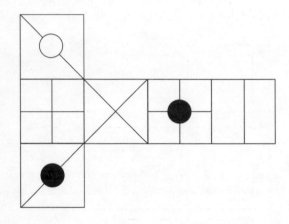

When the above is folded to form a cube, which is the only one of the following that can be produced?

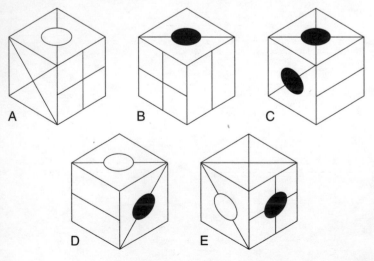

7. Between 50 and 100 people hired a private carriage for a railway trip, and they paid a total of £2 847.00. Each person paid the same amount, which was an exact number of pounds. How many people went on the trip?

8. Which word in brackets is opposite in meaning to the word in capitals?

PIQUANT (slow, tart, pleased, bland, irreverent)

9.

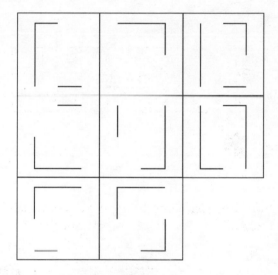

Which is the missing square?

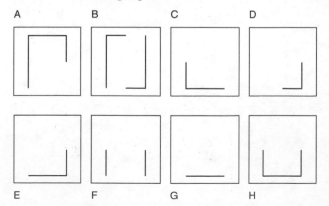

10. How many minutes is it before 12 noon if 70 minutes ago it was four times as many minutes past 9 am?

11. Downwards is to prostrate as upwards is to: supine, canine, doctrine, sanguine, cabilline

12.

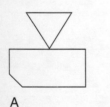

is to:

as:

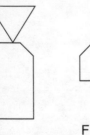

is to:

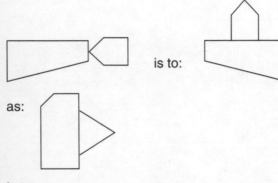

A   B   C   D

E   F   G   H

13.

586 : 46

374 : 25

Which numbers below have the same relationship to one another as the numbers above?

A. 246 : 48   B. 319 : 13   C. 642 : 20   D. 913 : 28
E. 832 : 26

14. Find two words, one in each circle. Both words appear reading clockwise. You have to find the starting point and provide the missing letters. The two words have similar meanings.

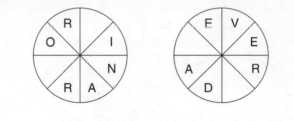

15.

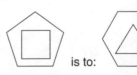   is to:

as:

is to:

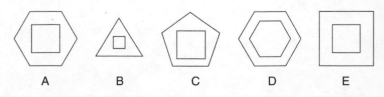

A   B   C   D   E

16. What number should replace the question mark?

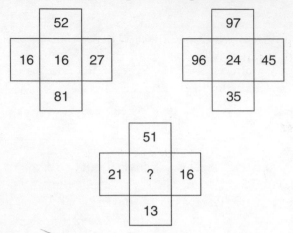

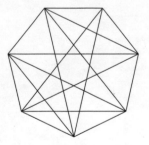

17. Place a word in the brackets that means the same as the definitions outside the brackets:

retain (   ) place for storing cargo

18. How many lines appear inside the heptagon?

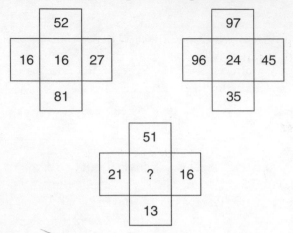

19. 23, 5, 28, 10, 38, 11, 49, ?

What comes next?

20. Solve the anagram in brackets to complete the quotation by Voltaire.

(inept force) is attained by slow degrees; it requires the hand of time.

21.

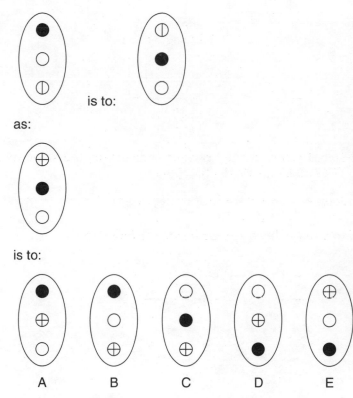

is to:

as:

is to:

A   B   C   D   E

22. 100, 10, 99, 11, 97, 13, 94, 16, 90, 20, ?, ?

Which two numbers come next?

23. Find two words from the clues provided that differ by the omission of a single letter?

locality / step

24. Which is the odd one out?

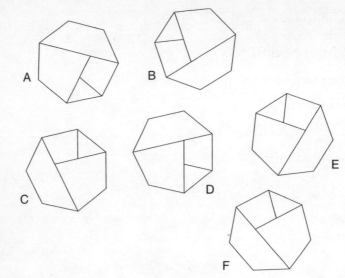

25. 1, 2, 5, 14, 41, ?

What comes next?

26. Which is the odd one out?

sector, region, district, land, area

27.

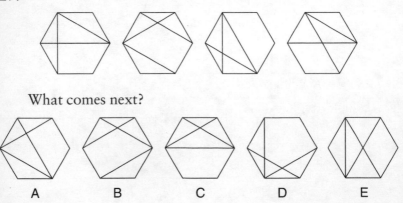

What comes next?

28. 27, 54, 81, 108, ?

What comes next?

29. What is a PIPETTE?

a. a small bird

b. a flower

c. a small bucket

d. a glass tube

e. a stalk attached to a leaf or stem

30. Which is the odd one out?

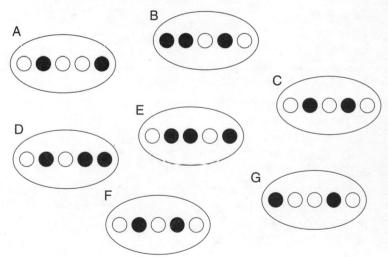

Answers to Test 1

1. £130.00. Originally Bill had £80.00 and Alan £50.00.
2. hedonism
3. D: the dot is moving down at each stage. When it lands in a figure, that figure is inverted.
4. 70: deduct 12 then add 3 alternately.
5. to mark time
6. B
7. 73 people pay £39.00.
8. bland
9. E: looking across and down lines are carried forward from the first two squares to the third square, except when two lines appear in the same position, in which case they are cancelled out.
10. 22 minutes
11. supine
12. E: the figure on the left changes into its mirror image. The figure on the right rotates 90° clockwise and goes on top of the other figure.
13. E: the second number is the first digit of the first number multiplied by the second digit of the first number, plus the third digit of the first number, ie 26 = (8 × 3) + 2.
14. ordinary, everyday
15. C: the number of sides of the figure on the outside increases by one. The number of sides of the figure on the inside reduces by one.
16. 10: add up the individual digits left to right and top to bottom.
17. hold
18. 10
19. 13: add the digits and then add the number produced, ie 23 (2 + 3) = 5, 23 + 5 = 28, etc.
20. perfection
21. D: the dot at the top moves to the middle, the dot in the middle moves to the bottom, the dot at the bottom moves to the top.

22. 85, 25: there are two separate sequences starting 100 less 1, less 2, etc, and 10 plus 1, plus 2, etc.
23. place/pace
24. E: the rest are the same figure rotated.
25. 122: multiply the difference by 3 each time.
26. land: it is a general term, the rest are divisions of land.
27. B: when two lines cross they disappear from the next figure and are replaced by two more lines.
28. 135: add 27 each time.
29. d. glass tube
30. E: A is G reversed, B is D reversed and C is F reversed.

Assessment

Each correct answer scores one point.

10–13   Average
14–19   Good
20–24   Very good
25–30   Exceptional

Test 2: IQ test B

Test 2 also consists of a battery of 30 questions equally divided between verbal, numerical and diagrammatic disciplines. A time limit of 60 minutes is allowed for the test. Calculators may be used to assist with solving numerical questions where preferred.

1. Which two words are closest in meaning?

    assert, ensconce, espouse, eschew, chaperon, advocate

2.

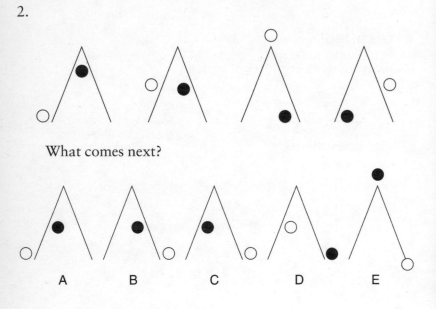

    What comes next?

    A   B   C   D   E

3. 100, 97.35, 94.70, 92.05, ?

    What comes next?

4. stet is to reinstate as caret is to correct, delete, gold, mark, insert

5.

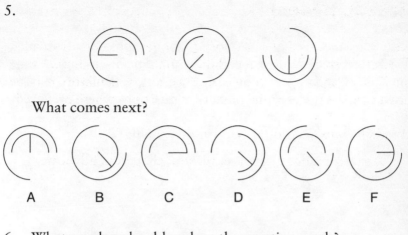

What comes next?

A   B   C   D   E   F

6. What number should replace the question mark?

7. Which two of these words are the most opposite in meaning?

rugged, diligent, critical, practical, indifferent, resolute

8.

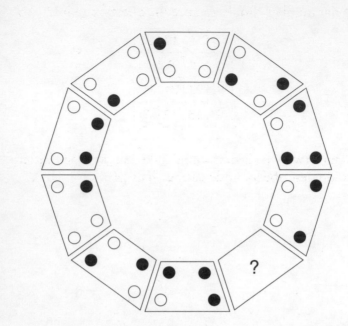

Which trapezium should replace the question mark?

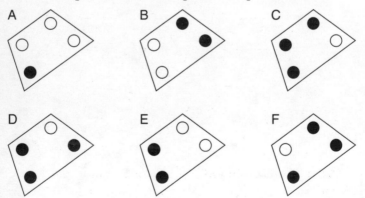

9. What number should replace the question mark?

14	18	17	22
6	12	9	16
18	22	21	26
9	15	12	?

10. Which two words that sound alike, but are spelt differently, could describe an undeviating channel?

11.

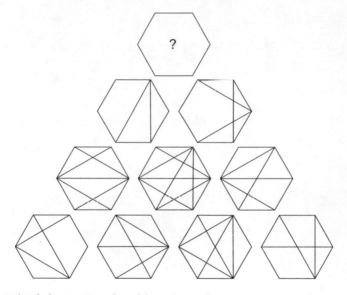

Which hexagon should replace the question mark?

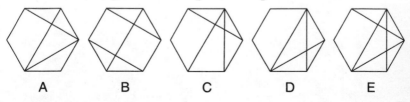

A   B   C   D   E

12. If a man weighs 75 per cent of his own weight plus 42 lb, how much does he weigh?

13. Only one group of six letters below can be arranged to spell out a six-letter word in the English language. Find the word.

URCIMA

KYCELO

OCTENI

MYEDCO

UDCMAN

ECAWLO

14.

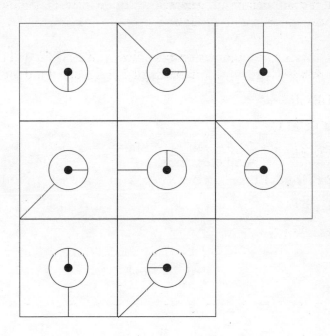

Which is the missing square?

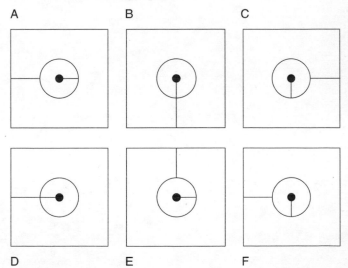

15. What number should replace the question mark?

16. Start at one of the corner squares and spiral clockwise around the perimeter, finishing at the middle square to spell out a nine-letter word. You have to provide the missing letters.

C	A	S
I	L	
T		E

17.

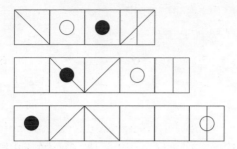

What comes next?

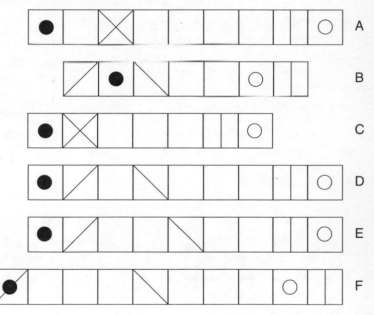

18. A man has 53 coloured socks in his drawer: 16 identical blue socks, 25 identical red socks and 12 identical grey socks. The lights have failed and he is left completely in the dark. How many socks must he take out of the drawer to be 100 per cent certain he then has at least one pair of each colour?

19. Insert the letters below into the blank spaces to create two words that are synonyms.

E C L L M N N R T U

* A G * * * I *   A * * * * I * G

20.

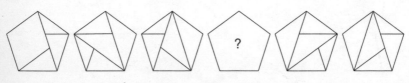

Which pentagon should replace the question mark?

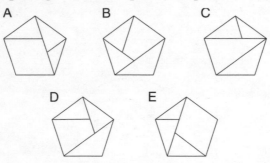

21. 1, 2, 5, 10, 17, 26, ?

What number should replace the question mark?

22. Conjecture is to speculation as dogma is to: delusion, conviction, consensus, evidence, opinion

23. Which is the odd one out?

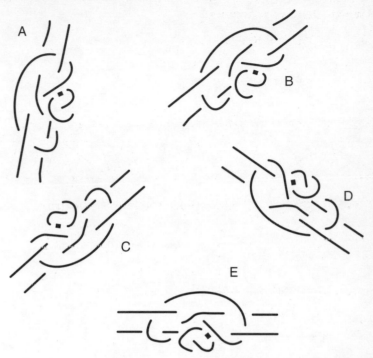

24. Susan has £800 to spend. She spends 2/5 of the £800 on clothes, 0.425 of the £800 on jewellery and writes out a cheque for £160.00 for a new watch. What is her financial situation at the end of the day?

25. Arrange the blocks into the correct order so that a familiar saying is spelled out.

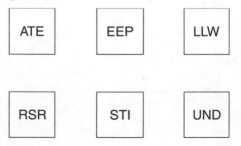

26.

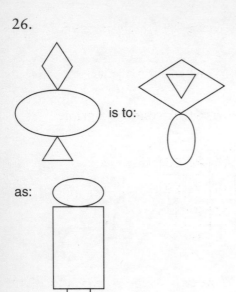

as:

is to:

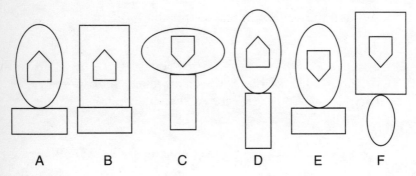

A   B   C   D   E   F

27. Identify a number in the grid which meets the two following simple rules:

i. it is not in any line across which contains a square number

ii. it is not in any line down which contains a prime number

19	15	22	25
32	18	7	29
26	27	4	14
12	16	39	2

28. If spacious heath leads to the palindrome 'roomy moor', to what palindrome does the clue burst forth flawless refer?

29. 100, 98, 94, 86, 70, ?

What number should replace the question mark?

30.

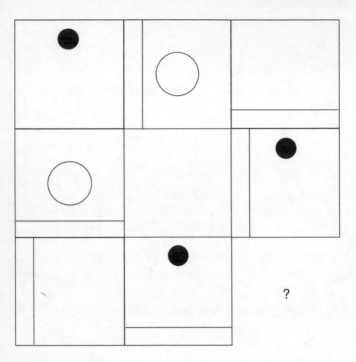

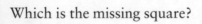

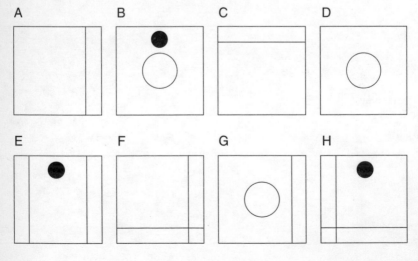

Which is the missing square?

A   B   C   D

E   F   G   H

Answers to Test 2

1. espouse, advocate
2. C: the white dot is moving clockwise round the outside, the black dot is moving clockwise round the inside; both move by an equal amount at each stage.
3. 89.4: deduct 2.65 each time.
4. insert
5. B: the large arc moves 90° clockwise at each stage, the small arc moves 90° anti-clockwise, the line moves 45° anti-clockwise.
6. 25: (350/7)/2 = 25.
7. diligent, indifferent
8. F: directly opposite trapeziums have black/white dot reversal.
9. 19: looking across, alternate squares are plus 3 / plus 4; looking down they are plus 4 / plus 3.
10. straight strait
11. A: the contents of each hexagon are determined by the contents of the two hexagons directly below it. Lines within these two hexagons are carried forward to the hexagon above, except where two lines appear in the same position, in which case they are cancelled out.
12. 168 lb: 75% × 168 = 126 + 42 = 168
13. MYEDCO = comedy
14. F: the internal line is moving 90° anti-clockwise in lines across and down. The external longer line is moving 45° clockwise in lines across and 45° anti-clockwise in lines down.
15. 19: (12 + 19) × 2 = 62.
16. sceptical
17. E: the diagonal lines are moving one square forward and one square back respectively. The white dot is moving two squares forward. The black dot is moving one square back.
18. 43 socks. If he takes out 41 socks, although it is very unlikely, they could all be blue and red. To be 100 per cent certain he also has a pair of grey socks he must take out two more.
19. magnetic, alluring

20. E: the left-hand three pentagons are a mirror image of the right three.
21. 37: add 1, 3, 5, 7, 9, 11.
22. conviction
23. D: the rest are all identical. D has a line which is upside down to the rest.
24. Minus £20.00
25. still waters run deep
26. A: the ellipse increases in size, and rotates 90°. The rectangle rotates 90°, reduces in size and goes to the bottom of the ellipse. The house rotates 180° and goes inside the ellipse.
27. 18
28. erupt pure
29. 38: deduct 2, 4, 8, 16, 32.
30. D: each line across and down includes a black dot, white circle, vertical line and horizontal line.

Assessment

Each correct answer scores one point.

10–13	Average
14–19	Good
20–24	Very good
25–30	Exceptional

Total assessment Tests 1 and 2

Each correct answer scores one point.

20–26	Average
27–38	Good
39–48	Very good
49–60	Exceptional

Creativity

The term 'creativity' refers to mental processes that lead to solutions, ideas, concepts, artistic expression, theories or products that are unique and novel. Because it is such a diverse subject in which there are so many different ways in which creativity manifests itself, and because in so many people it is to a great extent unexplored, creativity is very difficult to measure.

The creative functions are controlled by the right-hand hemisphere of the human brain. This is the side of the brain that is under-used by the majority of people, as opposed to the thought processes of the left-hand hemisphere, which is characterized by order, sequence and logic. If we were to remove a brain from the skull we would see that it is made up of two almost identical hemispheres. These two hemispheres are connected by a bridge, or interface, of millions of nerve fibres called the corpus callosum, which allows them to communicate with each other. In order to work to its full potential, each of these hemispheres must be capable of analysing its own input first, only exchanging information with the other half, by means of the interface, when a considerable amount of processing has taken place.

In the early 1960s the American psychologist Roger Sperry showed by a series of experiments, first using animals whose corpus callosum had been severed, and then on human patients whose corpus callosum had been severed in an attempt to cure epilepsy, that each of the two hemispheres has developed specialized functions and has its own private sensations, perceptions, ideas and thoughts, all separate from the opposite hemisphere.

As their experiments continued, Sperry, who won the 1981 Nobel Prize in medicine for his work in this area, and his team were able to reveal much more about how the two hemispheres were specialized to perform different tasks.

For most people the left side of the brain is analytical, and functions in a sequential and logical fashion. This is the side that controls language, academic studies and rationality. On the other hand, the right side is creative and intuitive and leads, for example, to the birth of ideas for works of art and music.

This is where the interface between the two halves of the brain becomes so important. In order for the subconscious of the right-hand hemisphere to function, it needs the fuel, in other words data, that has been fed into, collated and processed by the left-hand hemisphere.

Because it is so unpressured and uncluttered, it is in a young child that the mind is at its most creative, as the child instinctively uses both hemispheres of the brain, and learns an enormous amount of information and skills during these early years, without formal training. This rapid development can, however, slow down when the child reaches the education system, which generally concentrates on the left side of the brain. Thus, by the time the child has reached early adulthood the creative right hemisphere has been taken over by the more dominant left hemisphere – the hemisphere that controls language, order, sequence and logic – simply because the right hemisphere has not been given enough opportunity to function.

Because it is under-used, much creative talent in many people remains untapped throughout life. As in the case of many tasks, or pleasures, the majority of us never know what we can achieve until we try. Having tried, we instinctively know whether we find it enjoyable or whether we have a talent or flair for it. Then if these signs are positive, we must persevere. By cultivating new leisure activities and pursuing new pastimes it is possible for each of us to exploit the potential of often vastly under-used parts of the human brain.

We all have a creative side to our brain, therefore we all have the potential to be creative. However, because of the pressures of modern living and the need for specialization, many of us never have the time or opportunity, or indeed are given the encouragement, to explore our latent talents, even though most of us have sufficient ammunition to realize this potential in the form of data that has been fed into, collated and processed by the brain over many years.

The following exercises, while different in themselves, are designed to help you recognize to what extent you are using your creative talents, and hopefully strengthen your powers of creativity, innovation, generation of ideas and artistic skill.

Test 1: Imaginative shapes

In each of the following use your imagination to create an
original sketch or drawing of something recognizable incorpo-
rating the shape already provided. You have 30 minutes in
which to complete the eight drawings.

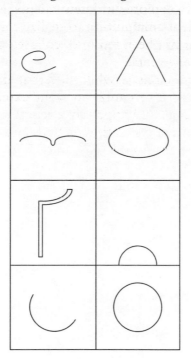

Assessment for Test 1

You can mark this test yourself; however, it is best marked by a friend or family member. Award one mark for each recognizable sketch, provided it is not similar to any of the other sketches. For example, if you draw a face, a second face scores no points as each sketch must have an original theme. You thus obtain marks for variety. If you are creative, you will tend to try to draw something different for each sketch.

There is no correct answer to any of the eight sketches as for each there is any number of ideas.

3–4 points   Average
5–6   Very creative
7–8   Exceedingly creative

Repeat the exercise as many times as you wish. Try other geometric objects or lines as a starting point.

Test 2: Creative logic

It is desirable to strike the right balance between right and left hemispheres in order for the brain to work to its full potential. This test requires a high degree of logical analysis, a left-brain function, but also involves a high level of visual awareness and creative thinking, a right-brain function.

In each of the following study the line, or arrangement, of figures and decide what pattern, movement or sequence is occurring, then draw what you consider to be the missing figure. You have 30 minutes in which to complete the 10 questions.

1.   Fill in the contents of the empty square.

2.   Fill in the contents of the empty square.

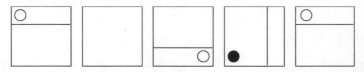

3.   Fill in the contents of the empty circle.

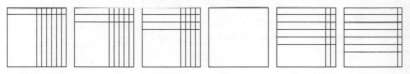

4.   Fill in the contents of the empty square.

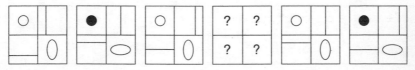

5.   Fill in the contents of the empty hexagon.

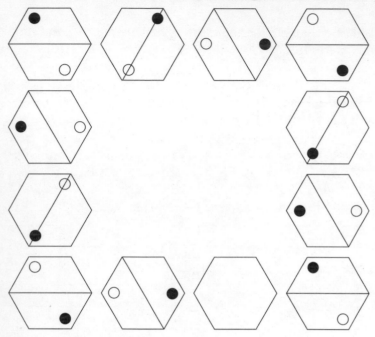

6.   Fill in the contents of the empty rectangle.

7.   Fill in the contents of the two empty squares.

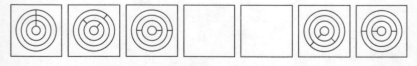

8.   Fill in the contents of the two empty pentagons.

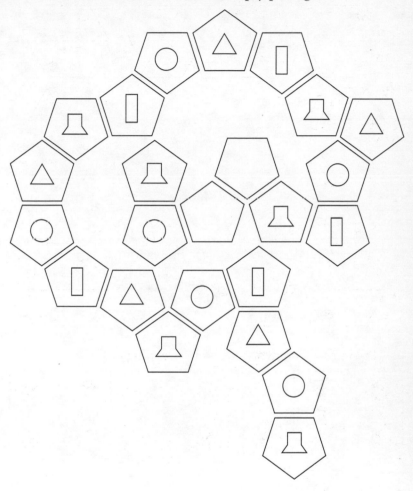

9. Fill in the contents of the empty hexagon.

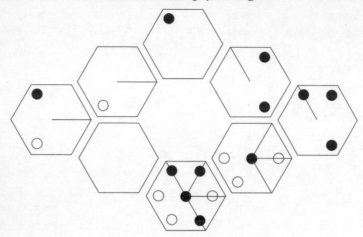

10. Fill in the contents of the empty hexagon.

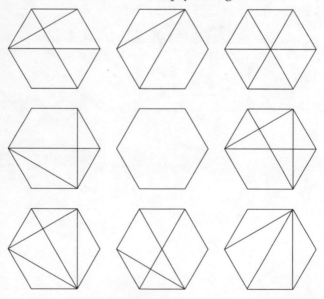

Answers to Test 2

1. The horizontal lines are increasing by one line at each stage, the vertical lines are reducing by one at each stage.

2. The dot moves one corner clockwise and alternates white/black. The line is parallel with each side of the square in turn, moving anti-clockwise.

3. The figure in the middle alternates diamond/ellipse and each rotates 90°. The striped half alternates top/bottom.

4. Looking across, the top left-hand corner alternates white dot/black dot, and the line in the top right-hand square alternates between three positions, as does the line in the bottom left-hand corner. The ellipse in the bottom right rotates 90° at each stage.

5. Looking all the way round the line is moving from corner
    to corner, as are the black and white dots. These are
    moving clockwise or anti-clockwise depending which way
    you look round the display of hexagons.

6. First the black circle moves down one place at a time, then
    the white circle does the same and finally the checked circle.

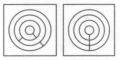

7. The outer and inner lines move 45° clockwise, the middle
    line moves 45° anti-clockwise.

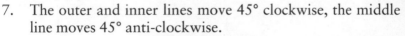

8. Tracing round the pentagons from the bottom the four
    symbols are repeated; however, each time they are repeated
    the chimney shape moves up a place until it reaches the
    end, after which the circle moves up one place.

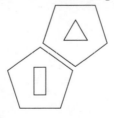

9. Starting at the top and working to the bottom, in each straight row of three hexagons, the contents of the third are the contents of the first and second hexagons.

10. Looking across and down, the contents of the third hexagon are determined by the contents of the first two. Lines from the first two hexagons are carried forward to the third hexagon, except where two lines appear in the same position, in which case they are cancelled out.

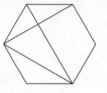

Assessment

3–4	Average
5–6	Above average
7–8	Well above average
9	Very creative
10	Exceptionally creative

Test 3: Imagination

The object here is to interpret each of the 20 drawings in the wildest and most imaginative way you can. You may also try playing the game with other people. The more wild you think someone's suggestion, the better it is and the more creative they are. Let your imagination run riot and see what you can come up with.

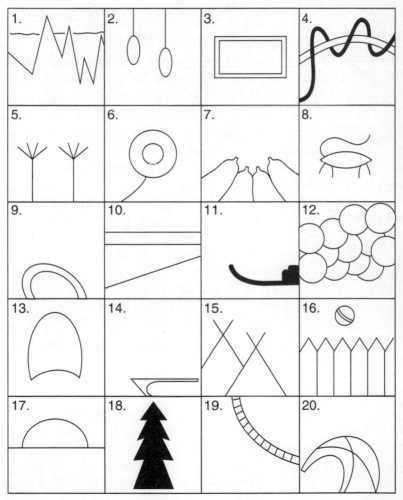

Test 4: Creative solutions

There are many different ways in which we can practise improving our creative thinking techniques. One of the main aims of these mind games, or exercises, is to break away from conventional and habitual ways of thinking and to generate fresh ideas, which can then be evaluated and the most effective ideas selected.

One such idea-generating technique, for example, is brainstorming, which can either be carried out individually or in a group, in which all the participants are encouraged to let fly with ideas and possible solutions to the problem in hand. Brainstorming is therefore a method of searching for, and developing, creative solutions to a problem by focusing on the problem and deliberately encouraging the participants to come up with as many unusual solutions as possible. During such sessions there should be no criticism of ideas, as the objective is to introduce as many different ideas as possible, and to break down any preconceptions about the limits of the problem. Then once this has been done, the results and ideas can be analysed and the best proposed solutions explored further.

Participants in such brainstorming sessions should not necessarily be experts in the field under scrutiny, nor should they necessarily already be aware of the problem under consideration. They should ideally come from as wide a range of disciplines and backgrounds as possible. This brings many more creative ideas to the session, and often someone looking at a problem from the outside may suddenly come up with a possible solution that someone heavily involved on the inside has not considered.

There are many other techniques that it is possible to employ either individually or as a group. Many such exercises may seem trivial, but anything that has the ability to put your brain to work in a different and novel way can have the overall beneficial effect of activating your brain cells and increasing your creative awareness.

The object is to put your mind to work in a different or novel way, in the same way that taking a different form of physical exercise stretches muscles which you did not even know existed. A few such techniques are summarized below.

What if?

Besides having great value in developing out-of-the-box thinking beyond what we know to be true, this exercise can be great fun. A thought-provoking subject for discussion is proposed, for example:

What if human beings were nocturnal?

What if pigs really could fly?

What if we all had the power to read each other's minds?

Divergent ability tests

These tests are based on Gestalt and Jackson's test of divergent ability, which requires the subject to name as many new uses as possible for everyday objects such as a brick, a 12 in square piece of cardboard, a bucket, a piece of string, a cardboard box or a towel.

Improvements to

Similarly to the above, this test requires participants to find possible improvements to everyday objects such as an electric toaster, a garden spade or a teacup. This exercise can then be extended to include suggestions for improvements to systems such as the motorway or rail network, and institutions such as the court system or the postal system.

Tests of creativity

The French mathematicians Poincaré and Hadamard defined the following four stages of creativity:

- Preparation: the attempt to solve a problem by normal means.
- Incubation: when you feel frustrated that the above methods have not worked and as a result you then move away to other things.
- Illumination: the answer suddenly comes to you in a flash via your subconscious.
- Verification: your reasoning powers take over as you analyse the answer which has come to you, and you assess its feasibility.

In the tests that follow a scenario is presented, and the object is to find the most effective and creative solution. Although the problems are timed, there is no assessment given. If you do not solve any of the questions within the time limit, it is suggested that you do not necessarily look up the answer, but instead keep it in mind and return to it later to have a fresh look. Sometimes a question that baffles you originally may suddenly appear soluble some hours or even days later.

Question 1: 15 minutes
A cleaner visits an office block that uses three lamps to illuminate the main reception area. They are all turned off and the switches are in the entrance hall, from where it is not possible to see into the reception area. Alone in the building, she goes to the entrance hall, uses the switches, then proceeds immediately to the reception area, where she is then able to determine which light switch turns on which lamp. How does she know?

Question 2: 30 minutes
When the subway was being dug under Victoria station in London a serious problem was encountered when water began seeping in. How was this situation remedied so that the work could continue?

Question 3: 10 minutes
Imagine a 3 foot cubed piece of solid metal anchored to the floor, with a hole drilled in the top, 2.5 inches wide and 2.5 feet deep. A ping pong ball is dropped into the hole. What is the easiest way to remove the ball from the hole?

Question 4: 10 minutes
A motorist encounters a flock of sheep travelling in the same direction as her on a narrow lane, and finds there is no room to drive through. The shepherd regards the motorist as a nuisance and wants rid of her, and the motorist regards the sheep as a nuisance because she cannot continue her journey. How is the situation amicably resolved to the satisfaction of both the motorist and the shepherd?

Question 5: 15 minutes
Using a candle, a book of matchsticks, a box of drawing pins and nothing more, find the most efficient way to attach the candle to a wooden door so that it throws out the maximum amount of light.

Suggested solutions to Test 4

Question 1
Put the first switch on and leave it for about 10 minutes, then turn it off. Put the next switch on. Go to the reception area immediately. The lamp that is lit is connected to the second switch, the one that is warm is connected to the first switch, and the one that is neither lit nor warm is connected to the third switch.

Question 2
The water was frozen, by drilling holes into the soil through which the water was seeping and pumping in liquid nitrogen through the holes, until the tunnel could be dug and cemented.

Question 3
The hole is filled with water and the ping pong ball rises with the water to the top of the hole.

Question 4.
The car stops and the shepherd drives the sheep back along the lane for a few yards to the back of the car, leaving the way clear for the motorist.

Question 5
Empty all the drawing pins out of the box and pin the box to the door with the drawing pins. Then stick the candle in the box and light it. This way, no wax drops on the floor, and the candle should not drop out of the box.

10

Memory

There are many different types of intelligence, and people who have outstanding artistic, creative, sporting or practical prowess can all be highly successful, in fact geniuses, in their specific field without having a high measured IQ. It must also be pointed out that having a high IQ does not mean that one has a good memory. Having an exceptionally good memory is yet another type of intelligence, and could result in high academic success, due to the ability to memorize facts, despite a lower than average IQ. However, someone with that rare combination of a high measured IQ, good memory, self-discipline, the right attitude and dedication is likely to be a very high flyer indeed.

Memory is the process of storing and retrieving information in the brain. It is this process of memory that is central to learning and thinking. Human beings are continually learning throughout their lifetime. Only some of this massive volume of information is selected and stored by the brain, and thus becomes available for recall later when required. Learning is the acquisition of new knowledge, and memory is the retention of this knowledge. The combination of learning and memory, therefore, is the basis of all our knowledge and abilities, and is what enables us to consider the past, exist in the present and plan for the future.

While little is known about the physiology of memory storage in the brain, what is known is that memory is not situated in only one part of the brain, but involves the association of several brain systems working together.

There are certain techniques by which we are all able to improve our memory, and while very little is yet known about the mechanics of memory, it is accepted that the more you use it, the better it becomes. It is therefore important to stimulate the memory by using it to the utmost, continually accepting different challenges and learning new skills. In addition to the enriching of our lives, this could also stimulate our brains' neural circuits to grow and strengthen.

The tests which follow are designed not only to test your powers of memory, but to assist you in improving your memory by developing your powers of concentration, and to discipline yourself to fix your mind on the subject being studied.

The remainder of this chapter consists of four practice tests of memory, followed by six tests which are timed and assessed to enable you to monitor your performance.

Practice test 1: Identification

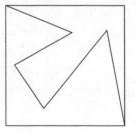

Study the above for 10 seconds then turn the page.

Practice test 1: Question

Which one of the following have you just looked at?

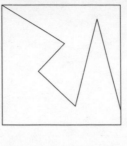
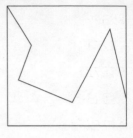

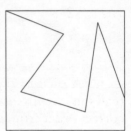

Practice test 2: Number order

462

8934

78261

958721

9154368

41262581

762135296

6824341752

Ask a friend or family member to read aloud each row of numbers digit by digit at a steady rate. After each line has been read out, see if you can then repeat the line of numbers in the correct order from memory.

Practice test 3: Recognition

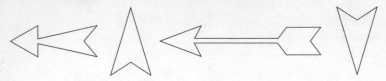

Study the above for 10 seconds then turn the page.

Practice test 3: Question

Which one of the following have you just looked at?

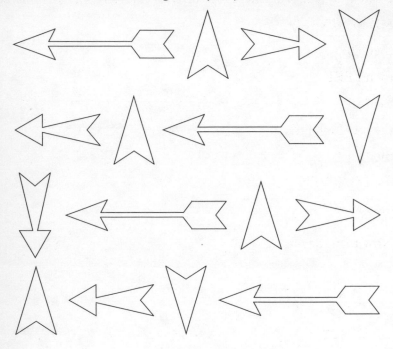

Practice test 4: Instructions

Read and memorize these instructions carefully for 60 seconds:

SIX to NINE

then UP

then LEFT

then UP

then to THREE

then UP

then to SEVEN

then to HOME

Now turn the page.

Practice test 4: Question

Which of the following is the set of instructions you have just looked at?

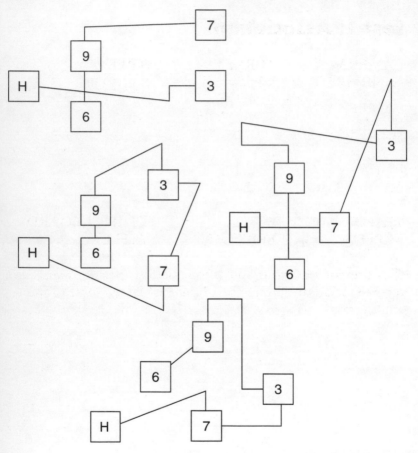

Timed tests

The following six tests are all timed and assessed.

Test 1: Association

CAMERA	TURKEY	TREE
WINDMILL	PIPE	MIRROR
PEBBLE	TELESCOPE	MEADOW
SCISSORS	CARAVAN	PAINTBRUSH
ROD	SPARROW	CARRIAGE
BRICK	WINDOW	RAINBOW
TEAPOT	BOWL	CLAPPERBOARD
RABBIT	BRIEFCASE	APPLE

This exercise tests your ability to remember pairs of words and form associations. Study the 12 pairs of words for 15 minutes and use your imagination to link each pair of words in as many ways as possible. Now turn the page.

Test 1: Question

Put the letter A against one pair, the letter B against a second pair and so on, through to the letter L until you have matched what you think are the original 12 pairs of words.

WINDOW..

PIPE ....

BOWL...

CARAVAN ....

APPLE..

MIRROR ....

BRICK...

WINDMILL ....

TEAPOT ....

TURKEY..

CLAPPERBOARD...

CARRIAGE..

CAMERA...

RABBIT...

PEBBLE...

MEADOW ....

BRIEFCASE...

SCISSORS ....

TREE ....

RAINBOW...

TELESCOPE ....

ROD ....

PAINTBRUSH..

SPARROW...

Assessment

10–12 pairs correct   Exceptionally good

9   Very good

7–8   Well above average

6   Above average

4–5   Average

Test 2: Memorizing an address

Study this address for two minutes:

Sophie Sisson-Fergus

Formisano House

38 Turnbridge Lane East

Hurstpierpoint

Cippenham

Hampshire

SH4 8TL

Now turn the page.

Test 2: Question

Fill in the 10 blank spaces to complete the address as accurately as possible.

Sophie ****** -Fergus

Form***** House

** Turn****** Lane ****

Hurst*********

******ham

****

**4 *TL

Assessment

10	Exceptionally good
9	Very good
7–8	Well above average
5–6	Above average
3–4	Average

Test 3: Names and professions

Study these names and professions for two minutes:

Joan Sparrow	Carpenter
Allan Taylor	Chauffeur
Frank Wood	Cook
Paul Driver	Ornithologist
Paulette Cook	Baker
Elaine Kitchen	Tailor

Now turn the page.

Test 3: Question

Complete the table with surnames and professions correctly:

A: Wood, Driver, Kitchen, Sparrow, Taylor, Cook

B: Tailor, Chauffeur, Baker, Carpenter, Cook, Ornithologist

	Surname (A)	Profession (B)
Joan		
Allan		
Frank		
Paul		
Paulette		
Elaine		

Assessment

10–12 correct	Exceptionally good
9	Very good
7–8	Well above average
6	Above average
4–5	Average

Test 4: Shopping list

Study this shopping list for two minutes:

tinned peas

frozen carrots

raspberry ripple ice-cream

Lancashire cheese

iceberg lettuce

onion rings

gravy granules

sugar

butter

strawberry cheesecake

Now look away, wait for five minutes, then turn the page.

Test 4: Question

Write out the 10 items on the shopping list. The order is not important.

Assessment

10	Exceptionally good
9	Very good
7–8	Well above average
5–6	Above average
3–4	Average

Test 5: Number grid

		2					7
		1			1		1
		3	6	8	2	9	4
					7		2
			7	1	4	2	
4	8	1	6		3		
			4	9	5	2	
			3				

Study the grid of numbers for three minutes, then turn the page.

Test 5: Questions

1. Which of these numbers can be found in a line reading across?

    127435, 2759, 368946, 4956, 368294

2. Which of these numbers appears in a line reading down?

    213, 456, 142, 819, 643

3. Which of these digits appears in the first column down?

    1, 2, 3, 4, 5

4. Which of these numbers appears in a column reading down?

    219, 783451, 6142, 127435, 68

5. Which of these numbers appears in a line reading both across and down?

    4816, 2131, 2743, 7142, 9173

6. Which of these numbers appears in a line reading across?

    6764, 7149, 4952, 5612, 8462

7. Which three digits appear in the second line across?

    111, 222, 333, 444, 555

8. Which of these numbers appears in a line reading down?

    7643, 8192, 3682, 8294, 8163

9. Which two numbers appear on the top line reading across?

    13, 17, 24, 27, 31

10. Which of these numbers appears on the bottom row?

    1, 3, 5, 7, 9

Assessment

10	Exceptionally good
9	Very good
7–8	Well above average
5–6	Above average
3–4	Average

Test 6: Attention to detail

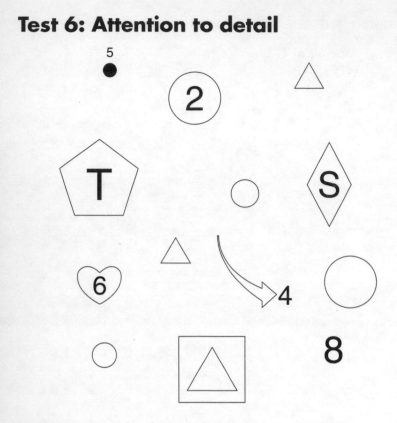

Study the above for three minutes, then turn the page.

Test 6: Questions

1. Which is the only odd number?

2. What letter is inside the pentagon?

3. The triangle is inside which other figure?

4. The arrow is pointing to which number?

5. How many triangles appear?

6. What number is inside one of the circles?

7. What letter is inside the diamond?

8. Inside which shape is the number 6?

9. How many circles appear?

10. Which number has a black dot immediately below it?

Assessment

10	Exceptionally good
9	Very good
7–8	Well above average
5–6	Above average
3–4	Average

11

Personality tests

'Personality' refers to the patterns of thought, feeling and behaviour that are unique to every one of us, and that distinguish us from other people. Our personality implies the predictability about how we are likely to act or react under different circumstances, although in reality nothing is that simple and our reactions to situations are never entirely predictable.

It is accepted generally that heredity and development combine and interact to form our basic personality. Many psychologists believe that critical periods exist in personality development which can leave a permanent mark on our personality. These occur when we are most sensitive to a particular type of experience: for example, when we are developing our understanding of language. A further contributory factor is how well our basic needs are met in infancy.

Although personality questionnaires are usually referred to as tests, they do not have pass or fail scores. They are designed to measure attitudes, habits and values, and are not usually timed.

There is no requirement to read through these tests first before attempting them, just the need to answer them intuitively, and without too much consideration. There is no right or wrong response.

Whenever you are faced with a personality questionnaire, it is necessary to answer the questions correctly. Any attempt to guess what you think is the correct answer, in other words the answer that you think your prospective employer wants to hear, is likely to be spotted when your answers are being analysed, as tests often guard against such manipulation by posing the same question more than once, but in a different way. At all times, simply follow the instructions and be honest with your answers.

Test 1: How self-confident are you?

Answer each question or statement by choosing which one of the three alternative responses given is most applicable to you.

1. How much do you depend on the approval of others in order to feel good about yourself?
    a. Very much, as it makes me feel I am doing right not just by myself but also by others.
    b. Not very much, as generally I trust my own abilities.
    c. Generally it does make me feel better when I have the approval of others.
2. How comfortable would you feel if invited to attend a social gathering such as a Buckingham Palace Garden Party?
    a. Not very comfortable, in fact extremely nervous.
    b. Very comfortable, and welcoming of the opportunity to meet many interesting and possibly famous people.
    c. Fairly pleased about the prospect of attending, but also a little nervous.
3. How often do you worry about your appearance?
    a. Frequently.
    b. Rarely or never.
    c. Occasionally.
4. In general, do you feel good about yourself?
    a. I often feel frustrated and that I could do better and achieve more.
    b. Yes.
    c. It is not something to which I have particularly given much thought.

5. How much would you welcome the opportunity to take part in a current affairs radio discussion?
    a. I would be very nervous and prefer not to take part.
    b. Very much.
    c. I wouldn't mind taking part, but would not be overly excited at the prospect.
6. How would you describe your expectations in life?
    a. I live more in hope than anticipation.
    b. Realistic.
    c. Quite high.
7. How good are you at selling yourself?
    a. Not very good.
    b. Very good.
    c. I have some strengths that I am able to emphasize.
8. Do you feel there is a need to conform in order to be accepted by others?
    a. Yes to a great extent.
    b. I am not interested in conforming, merely to be accepted.
    c. To a certain extent.
9. How important is it to live up to the standards of others, such as parents?
    a. I believe it is important to have role models.
    b. Not that important, as it is more important to become your own person.
    c. It is more important to live up to the standards expected by society in general, rather than the standards of individuals.
10. Do you generally strive for approval from every significant person in your life?
    a. Yes, generally.
    b. No, as this would seem to be an unattainable goal.
    c. Sometimes.
11. Do you believe you have the courage of your own convictions?
    a. Not particularly.
    b. Yes.
    c. Perhaps not as much as I would like.

12. Do you set yourself very high standards in everything you do?
    a. Yes, I believe everyone should set themselves high standards.
    b. I believe it is more important to set myself realistic standards.
    c. Perhaps in some things I do set myself high standards.
13. How optimistic an outlook have you on life?
    a. I am more of a pessimist than an optimist.
    b. Very optimistic.
    c. Fairly optimistic.
14. What are your feelings about trying but failing?
    a. Disappointment.
    b. At least I tried, now is there anything positive I can gain from the experience?
    c. Try, try and try again.
15. How easy is it for you to bounce back after adversity?
    a. Quite difficult, and there are some adversities from which you can never totally bounce back.
    b. It is easier to bounce back after some adversities than others, but generally I feel I can bounce back pretty quickly.
    c. It is never easy, but hopefully given time I am able to bounce back from most things.
16. How self-reliant are you in your own abilities?
    a. We all need to rely on others to some extent.
    b. Very much.
    c. Fairly self-reliant.
17. How desirable is it for you to develop personal standards in life?
    a. It is important to me that my values and standards have the approval of others.
    b. Very desirable.
    c. Fairly desirable.
18. Do you believe you are in control of your own life?
    a. Not particularly, and none of us are ever completely in control of our own lives.
    b. In general I am in control of my own life.
    c. I am in control to a certain extent, but not perhaps as much as I would wish.

19. How assured are you in your own abilities?
    a. Not particularly assured.
    b. Very assured.
    c. Fairly assured.
20. Do you accept yourself for what you are?
    a. No, there is always room for improvement.
    b. Yes, in general I do.
    c. To some extent; however, there are certain things I would perhaps prefer to change for the better.
21. How afraid are you of taking risks?
    a. I worry greatly about taking risks and the possible consequences of failure.
    b. I am not afraid of taking risks as this is sometimes necessary in order to be successful.
    c. It depends how great the risk.
22. Do you feel independent of the goodwill of others?
    a. No.
    b. Yes.
    c. Sometimes, but not always.
23. How do you view new experiences?
    a. With a certain amount of trepidation as not all new experiences are good ones.
    b. As opportunities to learn and open up new possibilities.
    c. As occasions where it is possible to either win or lose.
24. Do you carry out self-evaluation?
    a. Rarely or never.
    b. Yes, I often evaluate myself independently.
    c. Sometimes.
25. How often do you put yourself down?
    a. I am often very self-critical.
    b. Very rarely or never.
    c. Sometimes; however, I am also very mindful of the criticisms of others.

Analysis of Test 1

The three definitions of confidence are:

- assuredness and self-reliance in one's own abilities;
- belief in another person's trustworthiness or competency;
- an agreement that information is not to be divulged, as in the phrase 'in confidence'.

It is the first of these definitions, self-confidence, that is being assessed in this exercise.

Self-confidence is an attitude in which individuals have positive, but at the same time realistic, views about themselves and their situation. Such an attitude means that self-confident people are able to place trust in their own abilities and decisions. It also means they are able, to a great extent and within reason, to take control of their own lives and stand up for their own rights and aspirations in today's sometimes intimidating world.

At the same time, self-confident people have aspirations that are realistic. Being self-confident, therefore, does not mean being able to do everything. It does mean, however, that when sometimes their aspirations are not fulfilled, they continue to adopt a positive attitude and make the best of their situation.

Self-confidence also need not apply to all aspects of a person's lifestyle. Because self-confidence also means the ability to take a realistic view of themselves, some individuals will have total confidence in some aspects of their life, such as sporting prowess or social skills, but other aspects where they do not feel so confident, such as academic achievement.

Because they do not feel the need to conform in order to be accepted, self-confident people are not excessively dependent on others in order to feel good about themselves, and rarely put themselves down. Instead they are willing to risk the disapproval of others because they have such confidence in themselves and trust their own abilities, and are able to accept themselves for what they are.

Assessment

Award yourself 2 points for every 'b' answer, 1 point for every 'c', and 0 points for every 'a'.

40–50 points
Your score indicates that you are very self-confident and have great belief in your own abilities. Because you are so assured and self-reliant, you are someone who likes to be involved in, or take control of, any situation that concerns you. If, for example, there was a reorganization at work, you would want to take a central part in that reorganization and would see this as a career opportunity, whereas a less self-confident individual might view such a situation with a great deal of alarm and worry, and fear that the reorganization might lead to changes for the worse or even job losses.

The only word of caution to someone who scores so highly on this test is the need to be wary of over-confidence, to the extent that others perceive you as brash or cocky. You should at all times maintain a sense of reality, and bear in mind that success is something that needs to be worked hard for and will not just happen automatically.

25–39 points
You appear to be a generally confident person with a positive outlook. Although you are prepared to take a few risks in life, you are in the main someone who prefers security to a gamble. As you are not seen as over-confident, this means that you are able to interact with people on an equal basis, and this ability to interact with others is likely to make you a good team player.

You are likely to take a positive outlook in most situations, and have the ability to make decisions in a careful, measured and structured manner after weighing up all the options carefully.

Fewer than 25 points
As your score indicates a lack of self-confidence in your own abilities, you need to consider adopting certain strategies for

developing your confidence. This entails first of all analysing the reasons why you do not possess the self-confidence of others. One reason may be because it is simply the way you are. Many people are of a somewhat nervous disposition, or are so over-modest about their achievements that they tend to run themselves down.

There are other negative assumptions that individuals lacking self-confidence tend to make about themselves, which it is possible to address. These include:

- the belief that they are a failure, and not looking at the positive aspects of their life;
- the pessimistic attitude that disaster is always lurking around the next corner, and that even when things appear to be looking up and running smoothly someone, or something, is certain to throw a spanner in the works very soon;
- magnifying everything negative that happens out of all proportion;
- looking at others and thinking they have done better than you;
- taking a generally negative view about many aspects of your life: who you are, what you have achieved and what you will achieve.

Instead of adopting these attitudes, strategies that can be adopted for developing confidence include:

- Evaluate and emphasize your strengths. Give yourself credit for everything you try to achieve. Focus on your achievements and any talents you possess.
- Nothing ventured nothing gained! Do not be afraid of taking risks. Regard risk taking as not so much a gamble, but the chance to grasp new opportunities. Even if you fail, be upbeat and give yourself credit for trying, View the failure as a learning experience and as achieving some personal growth.
- Learn to self-evaluate instead of letting other people do it for you. Often lack of self-confidence is the result of focusing too much on the unrealistic aspirations of others

such as parents, or the standards and lifestyle of others in society. Instead, focus on how you feel about yourself and your lifestyle. This will make you feel more in charge of your own life.

- Do not expect perfection. There is no such thing. Learn to accept yourself with all your imperfections, at the same time balancing this with the desire to improve.
- Do not assume you always have to please everyone. Develop your own standards that are not dependent on the approval of others.
- Do not let your past rule your life. Develop the confidence to move on and make choices when circumstances dictate this is the best course of action.

Adopting the above strategies should have the effect of making you believe more in your own abilities in the future. If you can gain more confidence, it will in turn encourage more people to have confidence in you, with the result that you could become a more stronger, more respected person, and have more potential to achieve success in life.

Test 2: Success

Answer each question or statement by choosing which one of the three alternative responses given is most applicable to you.

1.   Which of the following motivates you the most?
    a. Life's rewards.
    b. My beliefs.
    c. My own personal desires.
2.   Which of the following words best describes you?
    a. Busy.
    b. Popular.
    c. Tenacious.
3.   What do you believe is the secret of success?
    a. To do something you are good at.
    b. To do something you enjoy.
    c. There is no one specific secret of success.
4.   Do you believe that some people are born lucky?
    a. Not really, as luck tends to even itself out.
    b. Yes, the finger of fate deals some a much better hand than others.
    c. No, as I believe you make your own luck.
5.   How easy is it for you to abandon good intentions?
    a. It is not easy, but sometimes it is necessary to move on.
    b. It is not difficult as sometimes good intentions can be misguided.
    c. I do not believe you should ever totally abandon good intentions.
6.   Do you go out of your way to impress the right people?
    a. Perhaps I have done on occasions and may do so again in the future.
    b. I hope I never would, as to do so is somewhat demeaning.
    c. Yes.
7.   Which of the following do you agree with the most?
    a. No one is perfect.
    b. Imperfection creates new experiences.
    c. Practice makes perfect.

8. Do you find it easy to keep focus on one thing at a time?
    a. Not particularly.
    b. I find it difficult as I like to diversify and have several things and interests on the go at the same time.
    c. Yes.
9. Do you know where you want to be in five, or even ten, years' time?
    a. I have certain hopes and aspirations but tend to live for today rather than forever planning for the future.
    b. Not particularly.
    c. Yes.
10. Which of the following words appeals to you the most?
    a. Steadfast.
    b. Sophisticated.
    c. Charismatic.
11. Are you doing a job, or in a career, that you really enjoy?
    a. I enjoy it sometimes but not always.
    b. No.
    c. Yes.
12. Are you a good loser?
    a. Losing does not particularly upset me, though I prefer to be a winner.
    b. Yes, as I accept there have always got to be winners and losers.
    c. There is no such thing as a good loser, it is just that some people show it more than others.
13. How easy is it for you to always finish what you start?
    a. I find it difficult to always finish every job that I start.
    b. I do not always finish every job that I start.
    c. Some jobs are easier to complete than other; however, I do always try to see every job through to completion.
14. Which of the following most represents your philosophy regarding hard work?
    a. It doesn't always bring all the rewards that it deserves.
    b. It is sometimes a necessary evil.
    c. Hard work is a means to an end.

15. Do you consider yourself as something of an opportunist?
    a. Not particularly, although if an opportunity does present itself it would probably be welcome.
    b. No.
    c. Yes, I am constantly looking out to grasp any opportunity that might present itself.
16. Do you ever long for the good old days?
    a. Not really, although certain things were better in what are termed the 'good old days', and it cannot be said that things always change for the better.
    b. I have many fond memories, and am often quite nostalgic, for times past.
    c. No, there is no such thing as the good old days and I always look to the future.
17. How confident are you that you can turn your dreams into reality?
    a. Perhaps more hopeful than confident.
    b. Whatever will be will be.
    c. Very confident.
18. Which of the following do you believe is the most important road to success?
    a. Possessing a high degree of skill.
    b. Knowing the right people and being in the right place at the right time.
    c. Hard work and commitment.
19. Do you have problems expressing your views and feelings to others?
    a. Sometimes.
    b. Yes.
    c. No.

20. How easy is it for you to change your job, or even your career, in order to achieve your goals?
    a. Not easy, especially if you are in a steady job that provides a steady income.
    b. It is difficult, as sometimes change is a courageous gamble and things might not work out for the best.
    c. I am sufficiently flexible to change what I am doing, therefore it is not at all difficult.
21. How important is the power of hindsight?
    a. It is not a total waste of time.
    b. It is of little or no importance.
    c. It can be useful.
22. How do you feel about having regular six-month appraisals with your boss?
    a. It is not something I would lose sleep over, though I would avoid it if I had the choice.
    b. It can be a distasteful process.
    c. It is something I welcome, as it provides an opportunity for career advancement.
23. Would you be prepared to give up your favourite hobby if it meant success in your chosen career?
    a. Perhaps.
    b. No.
    c. Yes.
24. Which of the following words best describes you?
    a. Wise.
    b. Generous.
    c. Ruthless.
25. Do you ever think you are in something of a rut?
    a. Sometimes.
    b. Often.
    c. Never.

Analysis of Test 2

It is said that the real secret of success is that there is no secret of success. It is certainly true that there is not just one secret of success: there are very many factors that, when combined, result in varying degrees of success for different individuals.

There is also no single definition of success, as what is considered to be success by one individual may differ considerably for another. For some people success is nothing less than being top dog and master of all they survey. For others it is a steady job with not too much responsibility and a regular monthly salary. Others may consider their main priority in life is a loving and stable family environment, and success for some is being one of life's survivors.

If the building of a successful career is one of your definitions of success, there are several essential ingredients in the journey to the top of the corporate ladder.

In the first instance it is essential to choose a career to which you are suited and that you enjoy. Having decided on a career, it is necessary to give it your maximum effort, be a team player, and be continually on the lookout to seize any opportunity which may present itself.

Successful people also set themselves goals. One common question at interviews, or at appraisals, is where do you see yourself in five years' time? Everyone needs goals by which they set themselves meaningful, yet realistic, challenges. Such goals, which can be anything you want or need, take you from where you are now to where you wish to be in the future, whether it is something you wish to accomplish that particular day, or over a number of years.

The setting of goals can only be effective provided you know what you really want from life, and take the action necessary to achieve your goals. You must also, if necessary, be flexible enough to change what you are doing in order to achieve your goals.

Keywords on the road to success

motivation, commitment, persistence, charisma, energy, resilience, adaptability

Assessment

Award yourself 2 points for every 'c' answer, 1 point for every 'a', and 0 points for every 'b'.

40–50 points

It is evident you do aspire to success, and that if you are not already a success in your chosen field you have the potential to become very successful in the future.

You appear to have the necessary qualities, such as determination and flair, and the right attitude and ambition to achieve the goals that you have set for yourself. And motivated by the desire to be very successful in your chosen profession, you are not afraid of hard work. The one word of caution to this is that you should take care not to become a total workaholic at the expense of yourself and your family, and ultimately your happiness.

It is necessary always to strike the right balance in order to reach most of the goals you have set out to achieve in both your personal and working life. If you do not strike the right balance, then one part of your life is quite likely to suffer at the expense of another.

25–39 points

Although you do aspire to success and have many of the qualities to enable you to achieve this, it may be that you need to instil more self-confidence into yourself to make you believe you can and will succeed. One way of achieving this is to remove any self-doubts that you may have about your abilities, in order to achieve the goals you have set yourself.

You should also adopt the belief that hard work does reap its rewards, and that some of these rewards could and should be heading in your direction. Having convinced yourself of this, it may be necessary also to convince others. This might not be so easy as convincing yourself, but it is certainly possible.

In general, however, it may be that you are in the happy position of being quite content with your lot, and do not particularly aspire to obtaining high positions in life. If your definition of success is a reasonable performance at work to provides a steady income and security for you and your family, then there is no need to change and set your goals unrealistically higher.

Fewer than 25 points

It would appear that power, status and riches are not the most important thing in your life, and you do not look upon this type of success as being necessary to achieve happiness.

If you do wish to make a success in your chosen career and reach the top of the corporate ladder, this is going to require a great deal of commitment and hard work on your part. But this effort will only be worthwhile if it is what you really want from life. Remember there are different degrees of success, and your definition of success, and the goals you have set, are what you require and not what other people require, or what you have seen other people achieve. Everyone, including yourself, should be their own person, as happiness is very rarely the result of trying to become what you do not really want to be.

Test 3: How content are you?

In each of the following choose from a scale of 1–5 (where 5 is 'most agree/most applicable' and 1 is 'least agree/least applicable') which of these statements you most agree with, or is most applicable to you. Choose just one of the numbers 1–5 for each of the 35 statements.

1. I have a loving and stable family life.

   5   4   3   2   1

2. I do not tend to complain a lot.

   5   4   3   2   1

3. I hope things will carry on in the future as they are now.

   5   4   3   2   1

4. I never wish I was someone else.

   5   4   3   2   1

5. I never vent my own frustrations on other people.

   5   4   3   2   1

6. I do not have an inferiority complex.

   5   4   3   2   1

7. If I have a problem I tend to analyse it and talk about it in order to find a solution, rather than complain about it.

   5   4   3   2   1

8. I am willing to adjust and change if circumstances dictate it.

   5   4   3   2   1

9.   I have a positive outlook on life.

    5   4   3   2   1

10. I tend to take things one step at a time.

    5   4   3   2   1

11. I find it easy to let things go.

    5   4   3   2   1

12. I usually get a good night's sleep.

    5   4   3   2   1

13. I rarely or never feel that I am stuck in a rut.

    5   4   3   2   1

14. I enjoy relaxing on my own for at least a few minutes each day.

    5   4   3   2   1

15. I never let things weigh on my conscience.

    5   4   3   2   1

16. I tend to define my own success path in life.

    5   4   3   2   1

17. I am not envious of other people's possessions.

    5   4   3   2   1

18. I must have been born under a lucky star.

    5   4   3   2   1

19. I have realized many of my ambitions in life.

   5   4   3   2   1

20. I never feel ashamed of things I have done.

   5   4   3   2   1

21. Other people's criticisms do not worry me.

   5   4   3   2   1

22. I feel relaxed and happy with my lot in life.

   5   4   3   2   1

23. I have a great deal of confidence in my own decisions.

   5   4   3   2   1

24. I rarely feel restless and wanting to do other things.

   5   4   3   2   1

25. I find it very easy to sit back and relax.

   5   4   3   2   1

26. I tend to focus on what is happening right now, rather than
     what has happened in the past.

   5   4   3   2   1

27. I laugh and smile just as much as most other people.

   5   4   3   2   1

28. I am never or rarely frustrated that I could do more in life.

   5   4   3   2   1

29. I never let little insignificant tasks annoy me.

    5   4   3   2   1

30. I do not feel frustrated that there is simply not enough time to do all the things I want to do.

    5   4   3   2   1

31. I would describe myself as a cheerful person.

    5   4   3   2   1

32. I really enjoy the job that I am doing.

    5   4   3   2   1

33. I am happy with my appearance.

    5   4   3   2   1

34. I greatly enjoy my leisure time.

    5   4   3   2   1

35. I have had many more ups than downs in my life.

    5   4   3   2   1

Analysis of Test 3

The definition of contentment is being satisfied with things the way they are. Human beings can only be guided by their own internal emotions as to whether they are content or are on the right path to contentment. Typical emotions are feelings of happiness or sorrow, satisfaction or anger, anxiety or euphoria. These emotions are either positive or negative, and it is the positive emotions that show whether you are on the best path to a contented lifestyle.

Contentment also means enjoying what you are doing right now, and not what you would like to do in the future. While it is important to set goals, and enjoyable to lookforward to things and make plans for the future, we can only be really happy at this moment in time. By enjoying the present we can also create a better future.Being content also means that we are flexible enough to realize that we are not right all the time, nor are we wrong all the time. Sometimes we have to modify our beliefs, or the way we do things. If we embrace change and move forward with it, this can be a life-enriching experience.

Contented people also have the ability to sit back and relax. They are likely to have a favourite place, even if it is just a favourite chair, the corner of a study, or a spot in the garden. This space then becomes their own fortress of solitude where they can spend some time, even if it is only a few minutes each day, at peace with the world and with themselves.

Positive keywords

satisfied, fulfilled, relaxed, light-hearted, vigorous, loving, dynamic, thoughtful

Negative keywords

frustrated, angry, insecure, exasperated, disappointed, tense, impetuous

Assessment

Total score 126–175

Your score indicates that you are happy and content, and have inner peace. This happiness is likely to rub off on those around you, especially your immediate family. For some people being content means that they are so laid back that they are accused of lacking drive and ambition; however, it is because they are so content, that there is no reason to change their lifestyle. They are content because they are their own person, and have achieved the goals that they have set for themselves.

You are in the fortunate position of having found your own niche in life, and are exactly where you want to be. Your attitude is likely to be the envy of others who have set their goals too high, and are frustrated that they cannot achieve their ambitions.

Total score 90–125

Although you are in the main content with your life, there may sometimes be the feeling at the back of your mind that you could achieve more, or have not fulfilled every ambition, and at times you may find this somewhat frustrating. Despite these feelings you would never want to realize an ambition at the expense of your inner happiness, or settled lifestyle, or your immediate family.

Your score indicates that in general most of your aspirations have been fulfilled, and there is no real reason to change, just as long as you continue to set yourself realistic goals, even though there may be others who are always keen to tell you what you should, and should not, do with your life. Always remember that it is your life, and life's goals only matter when they matter to you. Each one of us is the foremost expert in defining which path our own life should take.

Total score fewer than 90

It appears that in many aspects of your life you are somewhat discontent. For many people in the same position as you, this means that they have not fulfilled their ambitions or feel that they have not realized their full potential, or have not received the recognition from others that they deserve.

There could be very many other reasons for the way they feel. Perhaps they have set their sights and aspirations too high; perhaps they are in a job they do not enjoy, or are in a relationship which is going through a stormy patch; or perhaps they are just going through one of those difficult and stressful periods in life that all of us experience from time to time; or perhaps they are simply frustrated that life seems all too short and there is not enough time to do all the things they really want to do.

Even in such situations there is much in all our lives that we can be thankful for, and now might be a good time to take stock of all you have going for you. If you are able to focus on these positive aspects, there is every chance that the negative aspects, which in the past have been a cause for some despondency, will start to pale into insignificance. At the same time such a strategy should not be a papering-over-the-cracks operation, as it is at all times necessary to be honest about your current situation, and to diligently develop and implement a specific action plan to effect an improvement. However, any plan you do set out must, as ever, contain realistic goals, and must include a firm commitment to yourself to seriously carry out your plan, and be willing to adjust it if circumstances change.

Now you have decided on your plan and set your goals, it is time to think about the present and put any negative events from the past behind you. Only by adopting the attitude that what is done is done, putting bad events behind you, and focusing on the positive aspects of your life and your strengths that exist now will you be able to create a happier and more fulfilling future.

Further reading from Kogan Page

Other titles in the *Testing* series

How to Pass the Police Initial Recruitment Test, Harry Tolley, Ken Thomas and Catherine Tolley, 1997
How to Pass Verbal Reasoning Tests, 2nd edition Harry Tolley and Ken Thomas, 2000
Rate Yourself!, Marthe Sansregret and Dyane Adams, 1998
Test Your Creative Thinking, Lloyd King, 2003
Test Your Emotional Intelligence, Bob Wood and Harry Tolley, 2002
Test Your IQ, Ken Russell and Philip Carter, 2000
Test Your Own Aptitude, 3rd edn, Jim Barrett and Geoff Williams, 2003
Test Yourself!, Jim Barrett, 2000
The Times Book of IQ Tests – Book Three, Ken Russell and Philip Carter, 2003
The Times Book of IQ Tests – Book Two, Ken Russell and Philip Carter, 2002
The Times Book of IQ Tests – Book One, Ken Russell and Philip Carter, 2001

Interview and career guidance

The A–Z of Careers and Jobs, 10th edn, Irene Krechowiecka, 2002
Graduate Job Hunting Guide, Mark Parkinson, 2001
Great Answers to Tough Interview Questions, 5th edn, Martin John Yate, 2001
How You Can Get That Job!, 3rd edn, Rebecca Corfield, 2002
Job-Hunting Made Easy, 3rd edn, John Bramham and David Cox, 1995
Net That Job!, 2nd edn, Irene Krechowiecka, 2000
Online Job-Hunting: Great Answers to Tough Interview Questions, Martin John Yate and Terra Dourlain, 2001
Preparing Your Own CV, 3rd edn, Rebecca Corfield, 2002
Readymade CVs, 2nd edn, Lynn Williams, 2000
Readymade Job Search Letters, 2nd edn, Lynn Williams, 2000
Successful Interview Skills, 3rd edn, Rebecca Corfield, 2002
Your Job Search Made Easy, 3rd edn, Mark Parkinson, 2002